A Brief History of

Dr Joseph J. Morrow GMM
On the occasion of your
visit to consecrate
Lodge Lanna No 1852 S.C.
            Kevin Ralph
            Candidate 12/09/24.

A BRIEF HISTORY OF LĀN NĀ
Northern Thailand from past to present

by

Hans Penth

SILKWORM BOOKS

ISBN 978-974-7551-32-7

Published by
Silkworm Books
6 Sukkasem Road, T. Suthep, Chiang Mai 50200, Thailand
E-mail: info@silkwormbooks.com
www.silkwormbooks.com

Cover image by Silkworm Books
All photographs by the author unless otherwise noted.

Set in 12 pt. HP-Garamond by Silk Type

Printed in Thailand by O. S. Printing House, Bangkok

10 9 8 7 6 5 4 3

CONTENTS

PREFACE

Lān Nā or Lān Nā Thai ล้านนาไทย is the name of a region which corresponds approximately to the area of modern north Thailand. It is also the name of a conglomerate of Thai city-states in that area, and at times of a kingdom, which lasted for about six hundred years, from about 1300 to about 1900. Lān Nā extended its political and cultural influence far into neighboring regions in Burma, China, Laos, and central Thailand.

For the first 260 years, say from 1300 to 1560, Lān Nā was independent. Then came a period of about 220 years, until about 1780, when it was mostly under Burma and once under Ayuthayā. Thereafter it was allied with and a vassal of Bangkok, and eventually it became a part of Siam (since 1939, Thailand).

For about half of its history, say from 1300 to 1600, Lān Nā's capital was Chiang Mai whose ruler or governor was the overlord. After 1700 the Burmese divided the administration into East Lān Nā with the capital at Chiang Sän, and West Lān Nā with the capital at Chiang Mai. When between roughly 1780 and 1800 the Burmese were pushed out and Bangkok became the master, several of the former principalities became rather independent and formed two groups, East Lān Nā under the guidance of Nān, and West Lān Nā under the guidance of Chiang Mai. Since about

1900 all principalities have been fully incorporated into the central Siamese state administration.

The oldest known Thai document to mention the name Lān Nā is a stone inscription from Chiang Khòng on the Mä Khōng River, dated 1554. Here the name is spelled with the *mai thō* tone marker ล้านนา, meaning "one million rice fields." In the same inscription the name Lān Chāng occurs as an old alias for the city-state of Luang Phra Bāng, with the meaning "one million elephants." However, the toponym Lān Nā must be much older than that because it already appears one hundred years earlier on European maps, at least since 1448, spelled "Llana" on the Leardo map of that year, and "lanna" on Behaim's globe of 1492. The origin of both names, Lān Nā and Lān Chāng, is unknown, as well as what they originally meant or implied.

Several historical sources mention that Lān Nā was composed of fifty-seven *müang* "city-states, districts, lands." But the sources do not indicate the names of the *müang* nor the time in which Lān Nā consisted of fifty-seven lands. Perhaps in the course of time "fifty-seven" had become a mere conventional number, an attribute, which derived from some forgotten historical fact. The item of the "fifty-seven *müang*" was also part of King Kāwila's long new title that he received from Bangkok in 1802.

This *Brief History of Lān Nā* is meant to be of help to readers who would like to have concise information on the background of what is now northern Thailand, from prehistory up to modern times. But many details of Lān Nā's history are as yet incompletely known; much still remains to be extracted from written and material sources. That, together with the aim of this booklet to be a brief history, will make for lacunae and other deficiencies. Still, it is hoped that the reader will gain an idea of how the past became the present, and of what the present owes to the past.

Chiang Mai
May 2004

Map of Lān Nā and Vicinity

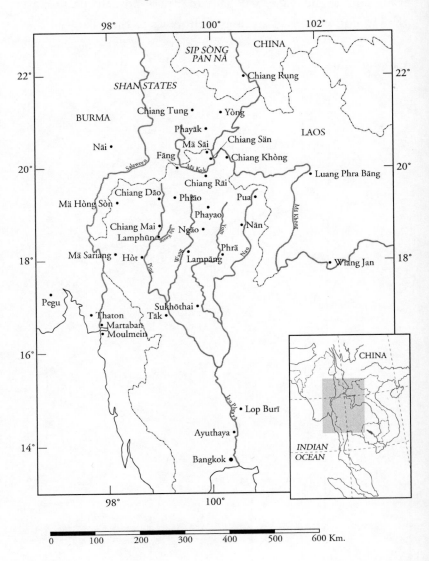

Figs. 1, 2. Two prehistoric tools of different sizes and kinds, from Lampāng province, c. 1,000,000–800,000 B.P. In the Chiang Mai National Museum. (1987)

Fig. 3. Later, more refined prehistoric stone tools, from A. Phrāo, Chiang Mai province. Said to have been found in the crypt of a stūpa ruin. Neolithic, probably 5000–3000 B.C. (1992)

Fig. 4a. Prehistoric rock-painting in yellow-red color in the rock shelter Phā Yiam Chāng ผาเยี่ยมช้าง, c. 42 km directly northeast of Lampāng. The larger figure is c. 67 cm high, wears a "skirt," and seems to be dancing (the "skirt" outline to the right has washed off). The smaller figure is c. 45 cm high. Neolithic, perhaps c. 1000 B.C. (1996) Fig. 4b. Silhouette or shadow drawing of the same painting. From หน่วยศิลปากรที่ 4 เชียงใหม่. ความรู้เบื้องต้นเกี่ยวกับศิลปะถ้ำ. Fine Arts Dept. Newsletter, 8.3–4, 2538 (1995), 24–28.

Fig. 5. Prehistoric rock-painting in reddish color in the rock shelter at Pratū Phā ประตูผา, about 45 km north of Lampāng on the road to Chiang Rāi. Two buffaloes are confronted by several persons. Neolithic, c. 1000 B.C. (1999)

Figs. 6. Phī Tòng Lüang (Mrabri, Mlabri, Yumbri) "Spirits of the Yellow Leaves." Proto-mongoloid representatives of an ancient prehistoric culture (hunter and gatherer) in Lān Nā. Reproduction from Hugo Adolf Bernatzik, *Die Geister der gelben Blätter*, Leipzig, 1941.

Figs. 7. Phī Tòng Lüang. Reproduction from Hugo Adolf Bernatzik, *Die Geister der gelben Blätter*, Leipzig, 1941.

Fig. 8. A Lawa. Reproduction from Gebhard Flatz, 'The Mrabri: Anthropometric . . . Examinations,' *Journal of the Siam Society*, 51.2, 1963.

Fig. 9. The Mon stūpa "Mahābalacetiya" or "Ratanacetiya" of Wat Kū Kut (Wat Jām Thewī) near Lamphūn, before its restoration in the 1970s. Repaired in c. 1220. Reproduction from Camille Notton, *Annales du Siam* (2), Paris, 1930.

Fig. 10. Mon stone Buddha image in Wat Sòng Khwä, in the former city of Wiang Thò, A. Jòm Thòng, Chiang Mai province. Approx. 1100–1250. (1973)

Fig. 11. Two Mon bronze Buddha images in repoussé technique from Wiang Thā Kān, A. San Pā Tòng, Chiang Mai province. Approx. A.D. 1100–1300. (1985)

Fig. 12. Mon stone inscription from Wiang Thò, A. Jòm Thòng, Chiang Mai province. When retrieved from the ruins of an ancient religious structure (cetiya?) in 1972, the thick stone slab served as pedestal for an unidentified holy image. The inscription has not yet been translated because it contains many unknown words. Approx. A.D. 1200–1300. (1980)

Fig. 13. Remains of a major irrigation canal dug east of Chiang Mai towards the end of the Mon period in about 1275. An example of early concern for infrastructure. (1968)

Fig. 14. The earliest known illustration of what was probably a Thai house. The structure rests on posts, an access ladder leads up to the verandah, and the roof is thatched. A cart arrives, drawn by a buffalo or cow/bull. The driver is standing on the cart. This picture was incised on a brick found in Szechuan, dated to the Han period (c. 200 B.C.–A.D. 200). Reproduction from D. C. Graham, 'The "White Men's Graves" of Southern Szechuan', *Journ. of the West China Border Res. Soc.*, 7, 1935; reproduced in E. Frhr. v. Eickstedt, Rassendynamik von Ostasien, Berlin, 1944, p. 193.

Fig. 15. The remains of Wiang Kum Kām, the predecessor town of Chiang Mai, seen from the east. Towards the west are Wat Kān Thōm, then the Jedī Liam, and Dòi Suthep in the back. (1975)

Fig. 16. An old type of Thai Yuan settlement: the former city (*wiang*) of Phrāo with triple earth rampart. It consists of two compartments which are interconnected by two parallel earth walls. Probably c. 1300–1350. (1976)

Fig. 17. Water lifting wheels, *luk*, หลุก, were often used for irrigation. Made of bamboo, the *luk* was erected in the river and was turned by the current. Short sections of bamboo, attached to its outer rim, lifted water above the level of the riverbank and poured it into drains leading to the field. A *luk* had to be dismantled before the annual rise of the river. This specimen stood on the east bank of the Mä Ping at Chiang Mai, south of the formerly iron Käo Nòwarat bridge which can be seen in the background. Reproduction of a photograph taken by an unidentified person in 1937.

Fig. 18. Base of a stūpa in Wat Phra Sing, Chiang Mai, with gold, silver, and bronze urns for keeping the ashes of King Kham Fū who died in 1336 or 1345. This is the oldest known remaining Thai masonry structure in Lān Nā; the urns are the oldest known Thai type of Lān Nā. The stupa base was opened in 1925; the urns with the royal ashes have since disappeared. Reproduction from Camille Notton, *Annales du Siam* (3), Paris, 1932.

Fig. 19. The Phra Mahā Thāt (Mahādhatucetiya) in Wat Phra Thāt
Hariphunchai, Lamphūn, in its final form since 1448. (1971)

Figs. 20, 21, 22. Head, fingers, and feet of over-lifesize Thai Yuan Buddha images in bronze repoussé technique; from the "bell" (aṇḍa) of the Phra Mahā Thāt, Lamphūn. Probably c. 1330. (1981)

Fig. 23. Probably in 1427 the ruler of Nān, Phayā Lāra Phā Sum, cast five bronze Buddha images. Four of them have been identified (Wat Phayā Phū and Wat Phra Thāt Chāng Kham, Nān, each have two). Three have square pedestals inscribed at the front; one has lost its pedestal. The images are either standing or walking and are slightly over two meters tall. They are the oldest known, dated images from the Lān Nā region, made at a time when Nān and Phrä were still in the orbit of Sukhōthai, roughly twenty years before they were politically integrated in Lān Nā. This image is in Wat Phayā Phū. (1986)

Fig. 24. Bronze image of the popular Mahāyāna bodhisattva Avalokiteśvara.
The damaged sculpture, c. 60 cm tall, was unearthed in 1970 when
the Montri Hotel was built just inside Chiang Mai's Thā Phä gate. It
supposedly is close to Ayuthayā images of c. 1400–1500. This find points
to a Mahāyā-nist minority at Chiang Mai (diplomats, merchants, artists
from Yüñan?). Indeed some of Chiang Mai's Buddhist art works at the time
contain Chinese elements.

Fig. 25. The main stūpa in Wat Jet Yòt (Mahābodhārāma), Chiang Mai. Built in 1487, it contains the ashes of Phayā Tilok. Restored in the early 1970s. (1975)

Fig. 26. (next page) Lifesize (176 cm) Yuan standing bronze Buddha statue, originally holding an almsbowl. Cast in several parts which had to be assembled. The "flame" atop the *moli* and the hands are modern wooden replacements. The inscription on the pedestal, partly written in Tham letters and Pāli language and partly in Fak Khām letters and Thai Yuan dialect, says that two monks and a lay woman sponsored the casting of the image in 1465. This is Lān Nā's oldest known Buddha image that is inscribed with Yuan letters. Wat Chiang Man, Chiang Mai. (1971)

Fig. 27. The Buddha image called Phra Jao Lān Thòng in Old Phrao, Chiang Mai province, cast in 1527 according to its inscription. (1969)

Fig. 28. A Yuan decorative brick from Old Wat Pā Däng (Rattavanamahā-vihāra), near Chiang Mai, where Ratanapañña in 1516–1517 composed in Pāli the famous chronicle Jinakālamālī. (1973)

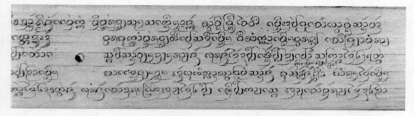

Fig. 29. Part of a palm-leaf manuscript of the chronicle of Chiang Mai, written in Tham letters and Yuan dialect; a copy made in 1926. This particular passage explains the choice of the little hill Dòi Jòm Tòng as *sadü müang* "country navel" of Old Chiang Rāi when that city was founded in 1263. (1987)

Fig. 30. Close-up of the writing on the cover leaf of a palm-leaf manuscript, copied in 1538. This particular passage reads (ปีเปิก) เสฑศกราชไท้ 900 ตัว "(in the year Pök) Set, (Cula)sakkarāja 900". (1977)

Fig. 31. (left page) The stone inscription of Wat Chiang Man, Chiang Mai, engraved in 1581 in Fak Khām letters and Yuan dialect reporting the restoration of the monastery with funds from the king of Burma. It is the oldest known document which dates the founding of Chiang Mai: Thursday, 12 April 1296, around 4 a.m. (1984)

Fig. 32. (above) The *bōt* (*ubōsot*, *uposatha* building), erected 1796, of Wat Phra Nòn, south of Pā Sāng, Lamphūn province. It stands on a little piece of land that is delimited by *sīmā* stones (which need not be beautifully carved as these here show) and is typically much smaller than the *wihān* next to it. (1973)

Fig. 33. Seal of King Phutthawong of Chiang Mai, attached to an edict of 1831 which gives special rights to a certain Lawa village. The seal shows an elephant with howdah; the decree is engraved on a silver foil. (1970)

Fig. 34. The earliest known photograph of a city gate of Chiang Mai (unidentified). The gate dates from the last thorough restoration of the city wall around 1800. The photograph was taken in 1899. The gate in this photograph served as model when Chiang Mai's Thā Phä Gate was reconstructed in 1986.

Fig. 35. A Thai Yuan monk. The late Jao Athikān Insuan Suvaṇṇo, abbot of Wat Phan Tao, Chiang Mai, on a visit to another monastery, Wat Phra Thāt Dòi Suthep. (1967)

Fig. 36. Old-time hygiene. Toilet with separation of urine and stool, from a monastery ruin south of Lamphūn. In the Lamphūn National Museum. Mostly these lavatory seats were made of wood and therefore have not survived; there is one in Sukhōthai National Museum. (1973)

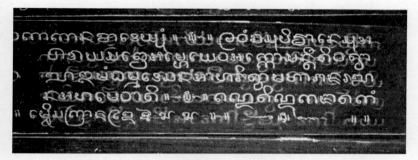

Fig. 37. The oldest known Lān Nā palm-leaf manuscript is a Jātaka book of 11 fascicles. It is written in Tham letters and Pāli language and contains the Vīsati-, Tiṃsa- and Sattati-nipātas. Fascicle 9, called *Tiṃsanipāta, Kusarāja-jātaka*, has on leaf *dhi* (leaf 27 verso) at the end of line 5 a short note in Thai: "[written] in [the year Cula]sakkarāja 833," viz. A.D. 1471/72. The reproduction shows that part of the palm leaf. The letters are deeply incised and so thoroughly blackened that they appear in reverse on the other side of the palm leaf. This is a white/black inverse reproduction. The manuscript is kept in Wat Lāī Hin, Amphö Kò Kha, Lampāng province. (1995)

Fig. 38. (next page) Bronze image of the *rüsi* (P. (isi) "hermit" Kamon (P. Kamala) of Dòi Tung, north of Chiang Rāi. The inscription (ALI 1.4.3.2 Dòi Tung 1605) contains the earliest known version of the Dòi Tung Chronicle and dates the image in year 1605. The sculpture shows how people at the time imagined a hermit of the past, thus also the legendary Suthep, founder of Lamphūn around 750, who had his domicile on Dòi Suthep near Chiang Mai which carries his name. A teapot with snout is on his right while on his left are a small basket container like those used by the Yuan for their glutinous rice and a pot or bowl. The image is 74 cm high and is now in the Chiang Sän Museum. (1985)

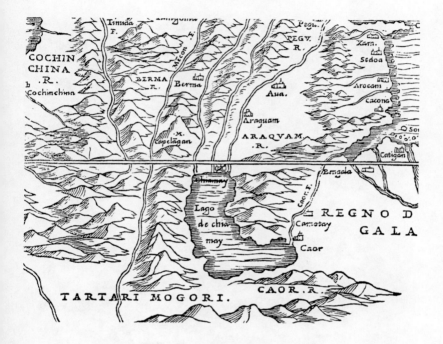

Fig. 39. Section of the original (woodcut) map of Southeast Asia by
Giacomo Gastaldi, printed in 1554 in the second volume of G. B. Ramusio:
I viaggi et navigatione. 3 vols. Venice, 1550–1556.

The map is drawn "upside down," i.e. north is at the bottom and south
at the top. The double line running across the map is the Tropic of Cancer
at N 21°26'. The city of Chiang Mai "Chiamay" is placed on the south
shore of Lake Chiang Mai "Lago de chiamay" between two of three rivers
that emanate from the lake and flow south. A later owner of the map neatly
crossed out the name of the city and the icon representing it, probably
because by then better or different information was available. The actual
latitude of Chiang Mai is 18°47', slightly more to the south ("higher") than
shown on the map. The lake is about 10 degrees long from north to south,
or about 1,000 km.

From: Thomas Suarez, *Early Mapping of Southeast Asia*. Singapore,
Periplus Edition, 1999, p. 153 fig. 79.

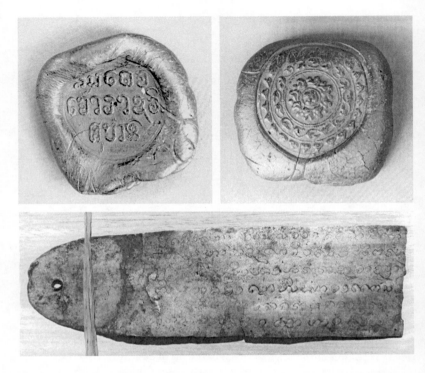

Fig. 40, 41, 42. Seal of Queen Wisuttha Thewī of Chiang Mai, front and back. The seal was attached to an edict, written on a silver foil. The two halves of the seal have broken off, and the silver foil itself is broken in half. The name/ title on the seal reads "Her Majesty Queen Wisuttha." The edict states that on Wednesday, 21 May 1567, the queen donated five villages, located in three forests, to the service of Wat Rācha Witsuttharām. All revenue from this area was to go to the monastery. The villagers were not to be used for outside or other work. The monastery bears her name and was obviously founded by her. It still exists in Bān Phä, A. Hòt, Chiang Mai province.

In 1632 this document was successfully used by the villagers to prevent King Sutthō (Talun) from deporting them to Burma.

Fig. 43. Monument of Phayā Thip Chăng in Lampāng province (?–1757), the first king of the Jao Jet Ton dynasty. (Silkworm Books, 1994)

PREHISTORY

C. 1,000,000 B.P.–C. A.D. 750

The Paleolithic Period
c. 1 million B.P.–12,000 B.C.

Lān Nā was already inhabited by hominids, i.e. human ancestors, about one million years ago. That was the beginning of Lān Nā's oldest prehistoric period, the Paleolithic (c. 1,000,000 B.P.–12,000 B.C.).[1]

In 1999 in Lampāng province bone fragments were found of what provisionally has been identified as *Homo erectus* "man who walks upright," viz. the first human being to evolve from ape-like ancestors. This Lampāng *Homo erectus* is dated between 800,000 and 400,000 B.P. and is placed geographically between two other *Homo erectus,* viz. Indonesia's Sanggiran II Man of Java and China's Peking Man, or *Pithecanthropus pekinensis.* The Lampāng *Homo erectus* lived in the mouth of caves near meadows and streams. His main natural enemies included the giant hyena, the saber-toothed tiger, the orangutan, and the giant panda.

---

1 B.P. = before present; B.C. = before Christ; A.D. = *anno domini* "in the year of the Lord" i.e. after Christ.

Stone tools found in geologically dated sites in the provinces of Lampāng and Phrä range in age from one million years to 600,000 years. Younger paleolithic stone tools have been found for instance in the cave Tham Phra on the Mä Kok River near Chiang Rāi. A typical paleolithic stone tool is the river pebble, sometimes quite large and flaked off, i.e. sharpened, on one side only.

In these early times, natural caves and rock shelters played a certain role in the life of the people. Towards the end of the Paleolithic, or geologically speaking in late Pleistocene times (c. 40,000–15,000 B.P.), caves were only used as short-time campsites and were not permanent dwellings; often the caves chosen were particularly difficult to reach.

The Mesolithic Period
c. 12,000–6000 B.C.

The stretch of time between the end of the Paleolithic and the beginning of the next period, the Neolithic, is sometimes called the Mesolithic Period, c. 12,000–6000 B.C. The tools dating from this Stone Age resemble other stone tools found in several places in mainland Southeast Asia and, together with them, form a material or technical, if not spiritual, culture complex called Hoabinhian, named after the village Hoabinh in north Vietnam where many remains of this culture were first found and studied.

During the Mesolithic, the life of the people underwent a great change. Many groups abandoned the earlier nomadic hunting and gathering lifestyle and took to a more sedentary village horticulture and farming life.

In the early Mesolithic, corresponding approximately to early Holocene times (c. 15,000–10,000 B.P.), caves were often used as permanent dwelling sites.

The Neolithic Period
c. 6000–600 B.C.

After the present climate had stabilized in the region, c. 10,000 B.C., there began a younger prehistoric period, the Neolithic (c. 6000–600 B.C.), which is characterized chiefly by five new inventions or technologies: improvement of stone tools by polishing the stone instrument for better cutting results (typical instruments in Lān Nā are the polished shoulder ax with a rectangular or trapezoid cross-section); cord and its uses, basketry and its uses; bark cloth manufacture; and pottery manufacture.

The domestication of animals began in c. 6000 B.C., probably first with pig and chicken. Wild rice became domesticated in c. 3000 B.C. The Neolithic was a time of increased food supply, in quantity, in quality, and in variety. It is easy to imagine that as a result, the general health of the people improved, that their life span became longer, and that the population steadily increased.

Younger prehistoric sites, in particular from c. 5000 B.C. on, are quite numerous and have been found all over the Lān Nā area, mostly in caves and under rock shelters. Also found were stone implement "factories," sites at which obviously great numbers of stone tools were produced, usually from schistic rock. One such site is the hill Khao Käo เขาแก้ว near Nān, where, lying over an area of perhaps three square kilometers, were found an estimated three million stone tools, mostly shoulder axes, or their broken pieces.

Occasionally, pious Buddhists of a much later age enshrined prehistoric stone tools in the chamber, *kru* กรุ, under a stūpa. The cave Tham Phī in Mä Hòng Sòn province is an example of a site that was used for thousands of years, from c. 12,000 B.C. to c. 6000 B.C.

In later Mesolithic and in Neolithic times, i.e. in the middle Holocene Epoch (c. 10,000–5000 B.P.) caves and rock shelters were often used as burial sites.

People using the caves and rock shelters occasionally painted on the rock. The neolithic rock shelter called Phā Yiam Chāng ผาเยี่ยมช้าง in Lampāng province has a yellow-red silhouette painting of two human figures. Not very far to the north, at Pratū Phā ประตูผา on the road from Lampāng to Ngāo, is a long rock shelter with over a hundred reddish images showing humans, animals, plants, and geometrical patterns, drawn with a paint based on haematite (Fe_2O_3).

The Early Metal Age
c. 600 B.C.–c. A.D. 600

The Metal Age began between c. 800 B.C. and c. 500 B.C. perhaps with the import of bronze objects, soon followed by iron objects. It is not known when local manufacture of bronze and iron objects began. Lān Nā possesses small deposits of iron and of the main ingredients of bronze, i.e. copper and tin, and therefore these metals could have been used locally in limited amounts, but it is still unknown which deposits were exploited when, and how much. In times of high demand, especially later in the Thai era, additional quantities certainly had to be imported.

There is no sharp time boundary between Stone Age and Metal Age because metallurgy was not invented or imported at a definite date and place and because people did not all of a sudden stop using stone tools. Even at present a modern Thai kitchen cannot do without the stone mortar. The invention or copying of metal technology probably took time to spread to all areas and all groups of people, so, in some areas some groups already manufactured or at least made use of metal tools, while others still did not. It is also likely that poor people for a long time continued to use stone tools because they could not afford the new metal tools, and possibly settlements of stone-using and metal-using people with different cultural backgrounds existed not far from each other.

Still, metal tools seem to have quickly become prevalent with a rather striking discontinuation of stone tools because in archaeological excavations, habitation levels with stone tools clearly underlie, and are separated from, habitation levels with metal tools. Occasionally stone tools were found in later burials, but presumably they were more a pious "parting gift" than evidence of the deceased person's actually using them. It seems that there are no known habitation levels showing mixed use of stone and metal tools. It may be possible to argue that the bearers of the stone tool civilization wandered off and that their place was taken by bearers of a metal tool civilization. But instead of thus having one civilization simply disappear into the unknown, and another arriving from the unknown, it is as logical to imagine that the same local population stayed on and simply switched from stone to metal tools.

Contrary to other regions on the globe, Southeast Asia, and Lān Nā, do not seem to have had a definite period of bronze-use, followed by another definite period of iron-use. Though bronze-making presumably preceded iron-making, it seems that in mainland Southeast Asia, including Yünnan, iron-making technology is not much younger, perhaps by only a couple of hundred years, and that very soon iron implements replaced bronze implements, though bronze items continued to be made (for instance, Lān Nā's later famous bronze Buddha images). It is therefore hardly possible to distinguish between a Bronze Age and an Iron Age. Since use of both metals practically developed side by side, the period of their quasi-joint beginnings is called the Early Metal Age.

The Metal Age continued a change in the old living pattern that had begun in the Neolithic. It added yet another specialized trade to make a living apart from the ordinary planting and animal raising, supplemented by fishing and hunting. The new specialties were mining, smelting, and casting or forging. Probably whole new villages were founded near metal ores or where metalwork was done; in other traditionally farming villages presumably one or several enterprising souls began trading in metal, or metal-working. Thus, since about 500 B.C., the settlements which once had been more or less of a similar aspect and occupation, began to look increasingly diversified: centers of pottery production, centers of mining and of metalwork, and ordinary villages with a few potters or metalworkers.

· · · · ·

During that long prehistoric period, there must have existed in the Lān Nā area many different populations, different people, different races, some following one upon the other, some being contemporaries. Correspondingly, there must have been many civilizations with different spiritual and material cultures.

But it is still impossible to describe the people of these civilizations, the races or the groups with their distinctive physical peculiarities and languages. Neither do we know what became of the prehistoric people. Did they die out, go away, stay on, evolve, and occasionally mix with later arriving groups, so that today's population are the far-removed descendants of these prehistoric old-timers? One suspects that perhaps all of these may be true to some extent. It is still unclear which early humans created or had which early culture. Only from protohistorical times onward, the period of transition between prehistory and history, does it become possible to match people with cultures and languages.

In the provinces of Nān and Phrä still live a protomongoloid people who until about 1950 had an ancient prehistoric-type culture of the hunter-gatherer kind. These are the Mlabri (Mrabri, Yumbri) as they call themselves, or Phī Tòng Lüang ผีตองเหลือง"Spirits of the Yellow Leaves" as they are known in Thai. But it is unknown whether they are descended from local prehistoric old-timers or are more recent immigrants. Some groups have also been reported in Laos.

Probably descended from younger local prehistoric peoples are the various Khā and Thin (Htin) groups with a simple gathering and gardening culture, and the Lawa (Lawā ละว้า, Lua ลัวะ)[2] who besides their gathering and gardening culture also have a traditional knowledge of iron working. Nowadays, in particular the Lawa are as modern as the average upcountry Thai.

The languages of all these groups—the Mlabri, Khā, Thin, and Lawa—belong to the Mon-Khmer type, the main subdivision of the Austro-Asiatic language family. The Lawa have been called the simple upcountry cousins of the more sophisticated Mon because they share with the Mon a number of linguistic, racial, and cultural similarities.

---

2 Not to be confused with the Lāo ลาว, as in "Laos," who are ethnically Thai.

LEGENDARY HISTORY
C. 500–C. 1200

Besides Lān Nā's factual history, there is also a popular, well-established mythical and legendary history which begins well before the presumably earliest historical arrival of the Mon and Thais, i.e. long before A.D. 500–800, and which frequently involves, quite unhistorically, a local Thai population at this early stage.

If this legendary history can at all be compared with Lān Nā's factual history, much of it would fall in the time from the end of prehistory to the end of protohistory, or approximately between A.D. 500 and 1200.

The area of present Mä Sāi - Dòi Tung - Chiang Sän is the earliest scene of reported events, from as early as the time of the Buddha Gotama (623–544 or 543 B.C. according to local tradition) who is said to have visited here, and even from before his time.[1] The accounts deal with kings and princes, Jong, Singhonti, Suwanna Kham Däng, Phang, Achutta, and Jüang, to name only some, with their achievements and wanderings, their quarrels notably with Khòm (Mon / Khmer) and Käo (Vietnamese), and

---

[1] The historical Buddha certainly never visited here. He lived around 350 B.C. in what is now northernmost India and just across the border in Nepal, and became not quite eighty years old.

they mention settlements such as Umōng Selā, Suwanna Khōm Kham, and Wiang Sī Tuang. But these accounts are of unknown origin and age. Since some of the events manifestly cannot have taken place (such as visits of the Buddha), since most personal names are otherwise unknown and since many toponyms and places do not seem to match the region of Chiang Sän, at least some of the stories must be regarded as folklore or legends which were brought from the outside and were adapted locally. The town of Chiang Sän, which often appears in these tales under a modified name such as Chāng Sän ช้างแส่น, actually was founded only in 1327 though likely it was not the very first settlement in that region.[2] Thus, the tales may go back to real events that, however, presumably took place between c. A.D. 900 and 1200 and at least in part happened outside the Chiang Sän area.

Of particular interest here is the general area of the mountain Dòi Tung - Mä Sāi - Chiang Sän which in legends or myth-chronicles appears under the names of Müang Ngön Yāng, Müang Yāng Ngön, Müang Rāo, or Müang Lāo. It is the place where the first Thai Yuan under King Lāo Jong descended from heaven, and where twenty-five generations later, now in fully historical times, Phayā Mang Rāi founded Chiang Rāi in 1263 before he founded Chiang Mai in 1296.

Another area that, according to legends or myths, was settled at an unspecified early time, was the region of Chiang Mai. A "foreign" Thai prince, Suwanna Kham Däng, immigrated in pursuit

---

2 Humans have been living in the area since mesolithic times, c. 13,000 B.P., as is attested by stone tools and other artifacts found here.

of a stag, founded a town at the site of Chiang Mai, and finally
went to live with a female spirit in Dòi Āng Salong (today called
Dòi Chiang Dāo), becoming a fatherly patron of the region and
also an ancestor spirit, *phī pū yā* ผีปู่ย่า.

Also the Lamphūn region appears in an early-time legend. The
Buddha had come here and had prophesied the future existence
of the city. A hermit or *rüsī* (*ṛṣi, rishi, isî*) later traced the outline
and founded the city. The legend manifestly borrows from ancient
Brahmanical and Buddhist sources; for instance, the outline of the
city is of the oyster-mouth type, an old Indian ideal town-layout,
and the name of the hermit is Suthep, or Vāsudeva, originally an
Indian Brahmanical hero.

Some of the tales are of considerable interest for early Thai
history in general and the early history of Lān Nā in particular.
These legends or myths differentiate between the origin of the
Thai rulers or of the Thai ruling group, and the origin of the
common people. One type of stories says that the (Thai) princes
came down from heaven between c. A.D. 570 and 640 when the
population was already in place; the origin of the common people
either is not explained or they are said to have emerged from one
or more pumpkins.

According to a well-known legend in Lān Nā, the first Thais,
or the first Thai princes, originally were a pair of gods (*devatā*),
husband and wife, whose time in heaven was expiring and who
were about to be reborn in the human world. Phayā In (god Indra,
Sakka), lord of Tāvatiṃsa heaven, sent them to become king over
this country which had no king but which was already inhabited
by an unspecified people. They arrived at Dòi Tung mountain,

north of Chiang Rāi, descending from heaven on silver stairs with their retinue of followers. After their arrival, the stairs disappeared into the air and contact with heaven was lost. The god-husband became king under the name of Lāo Jong.[3]

According to another type of stories, the princes were hatched from eggs the size of coconuts that had been found in the forest; such was the origin of the Pua dynasty whose later kings founded, and moved to, Nān.

Similar etiological or origin-explaining stories, with or without Buddhist elements, are known from Thai groups in Laos and Vietnam. For Lān Nā, the stories indicate that at one time Thais arrived from abroad and overlaid an indigenous population.

---

3 Similarly, from the Sukhōthai region is known the story of a goddess (*devadhīta*) who met a local man in the forest. They had a son who later, as King Roca or Sī Intharāthit, became the first Thai ruler of Sukhōthai, perhaps in the decades around 1220.

PROTOHISTORY
c. 750–c. 1200

The Mon Era, c. 750–c. 1200

The Mon of Lamphūn (Hariphunchai)
c. 750–c. 1200

Early history in Lān Nā begins in the Lamphūn region. Here, iron implements and unglazed pottery have been found in human burial sites, dated to between 300 B.C. and A.D. 100. Since then, the Lamphūn area has a proved, continuous record of habitation. The earliest population mentioned in the chronicles are the Lawa.

In the Lamphūn area Lān Nā's first advanced or higher culture developed, i.e. a culture that used writing and had an administration which reached beyond local villages.

In about 750 the *rüsī* ฤาษี "hermit" Suthep,[1] of unknown origin, founded the town Hariphunchai, modern Lamphūn,[2] on the west

---

1 S. *ṛṣi, rishi*; P. *isi*. He is also called Sudeva, Vāsudeva. The hill west of Chiang Mai carries his name, Dòi Suthep.

2 Tradition, based on various chronicles, offers many different dates for the founding of Lamphūn, one as early as 88 B.C. The date is found in the Chiang Mai Chronicle and in the Nān Chronicle. Both indicate the year 456 of an unnamed era which, according to the context, is an era based on the *nibbāna* of

bank of the Mä Ping River on a spot where it was believed the Buddha had once rested during his travels. The river changed its bed after 1500 and now flows about 10 km west of the city; at present, Lamphūn is located on the Mä Kuang, a little tributary in the large former bed of the Mä Ping.

The hermit invited the Mon princess Jām Thewī, daughter of the king of Lop Burī in present central Thailand, to become the new city's first ruler. Lop Burī then was part of the extended Mon kingdom of Dvāravatī (c. 500–1100).

The princess brought with her a good number of monks and craftsmen. The monks represented a Theravāda Buddhism whose canon, the Tipiṭaka, seems to have originated in south India, and whose sacred texts were written in the Pāli language. According to old traditions, the Mon had become Buddhists when two Indian monks, Soṇa and Uttara, sent by King Aśoka himself, arrived to teach Buddhism in Southeast Asia (Suvaṇṇabhūmi). That, it is thought, was about 250 years after the death of the Buddha, in about 300 B.C.

By about A.D. 750, when Lamphūn was founded, the religion of the Mon was mixed with some Mahāyāna-like ideas about, for instance, the magic efficiency of selected religious texts (*paritta, gāthā*). Presumably some Brahmin were also among the group who

the Buddha (Nibbānasakkarāja, a predecessor of the present Buddha-sakkarāja). The first year of that era was 544 B.C., thus 544–456 = B.C. 88.

The Thai Yuan usually name the year A.D. 661, which date is based on the chronicle Jinakālamālī.

Modern scholarship prefers the decades around A.D. 750. Indeed one chronicle, History of Nāng Jām Thewī, has a date equivalent to A.D. 767.

came north with the princess, and a number of the monks and laics would have had knowledge of Brahmanical sciences such as medicine, and calendar computations. The spiritual and material culture of the Dvāravatī Mon, brought by a royal scion and her group, thus reached Lān Nā by invitation rather than through traders and certainly not by warlike expansion.

The princess, who was married to one of her father's vassals, arrived without her husband. She was duly enthroned by the hermit. Soon after her arrival she gave birth to twins. The older one, Mahanta Yot, became her successor in Lamphūn. For the younger one, Inthawòn or Ananta Yot, another local hermit founded Khelāng, the predecessor town of modern Lampāng. Lamphūn and Lampāng thus were contemporary city-states, founded by locals for the Mon, and were ruled from the beginning by Mon kings. But Lampāng is hardly mentioned during Lān Nā's entire Mon era, does not seem to have Mon inscriptions or many old Mon artifacts, and therefore probably led a quiet existence; the leading city was Lamphūn.

Legend has it that the Lāwa king Wilangkha fell in love with Jām Thewī, wished to marry her, but was refused. This led to a war in which the Lāwa tried to seize Lamphūn but were defeated by the queen's two sons with the Lamphūn army. Love with problems between two high-ranking aristocrats, now as then is fertile literary ground, and so the story of Jām Thewī and Wilangkha has survived to our times in many tales with wide variations.

After relating the founding of the two city-states, our sources are quiet for the next two hundred years. In the decades around 950, two *milakkha* "barbarian" kings, of unidentified origin, were able to seize the city and usurp the throne for a period of time.

Next came the first of Lamphūn's two wars with Lop Burī, its parent town. Lop Burī had become a Khmer vassal between c. 1005 and 1022, during the time of King Sūryavarman I (r. 1002–1049). For unknown reasons, the two cities attacked each other repeatedly, the Lamphūn army going down or the Khmer-Mon army coming up, but neither side could overcome the other. Possibly Lamphūn tried to assist Lop Burī or to resist Khmer expansion, while the Khmer tried to extend their empire up to Lamphūn.

The two cities are at a distance of about 450 km in a straight line, and the battles, as they were, took place at the city defenses, not at places in between. Clearly, the intermediate territory was sparsely inhabited and did not yet have towns with a significant population.

The first war consisted of two campaigns during c. 1010–c. 1020. It began with the Lamphūn king attacking Lop Burī. But while both sides were preparing for battle outside Lop Burī, a third army appeared on boats, bringing the Khmer king Jīvaka from Nakhòn Sī Thamma Rāt (in present south Thailand) who quickly seized Lop Burī. The two Mon kings fled upriver to Lamphūn. The Lop Burī king arrived first and shut the gates. He married the queen of his rival, the former Lamphūn king, who returned south and whose further fate is not reported.

Three years later, the successor or the son of the new Lop Burī king called Kambojarāja "king of (the) Kamboja(s)" came up and attacked Lamphūn. In Lān Nā writings, *Kamboja* or *Khòm* means, not the Khmer of Cambodia, but the khmerized Mon of Lop Burī. Though Kambojarāja could not take the city, the threat must have been grave because a chronicle expressly mentions that the king of Lamphūn felt very relieved, greatly honored the spirits and ghosts, and asked them to protect the city from the Kambojas.

Even if these events were not exactly as they have come down to us in the chronicles, the essence seems credible and it is possible that this Kambojarāja was the famous Khmer king Sūryavarman I himself who unsuccessfully tried to add Lamphūn to his empire.

Incidently, this episode permits a glimpse at the popular religion then practiced by the Mon at Lamphūn, which included all kinds of ghosts and spirits and obviously was not free of earlier animistic notions—something still found today in north Thailand.

In around 1050 a cholera epidemic forced the Lamphūn Mon to emigrate for about six years to Mon towns in south-central Burma, first to Thaton where they were harassed by a Burmese king from Pagan, and then to nearby Pegu where the locals spoke a language very similar to their own and where many chose to settle and marry.

After their return to Lamphūn, the two Mon groups stayed in contact. The Lamphūn Mon once a year floated ceremonial presents downriver to their faraway relatives, perhaps a variant form of the modern Lòi Krathong ceremony. These floating presents must have been an abstract, ceremonial gift because, apart from the great distance, the towns were on different river systems. Also, Burmese Mon often emigrated to Lān Nā when in difficulties at home. The last major influx of thousands of Mon occurred in the early nineteenth century, but in 1815 King Rāma II asked his vassal, King Kāwila of Chiang Mai, to send them down to central Thailand and they were settled near Bangkok. Even today there are old people in the Lamphūn area who speak Mon and whose parents or grandparents immigrated in about 1910.

Lamphūn then may have been a renowned center of learning that attracted students even from abroad. The Burmese chronicle Pagan Yazawinthit พุกามราชวงศ์ says that when in 1084 the soon-to-become king Kyanzittha of Pagan (1084–1112) mustered his troops, he had them blessed with magic by a wizard who had studied here; he probably was a heretic Ari monk.

Soon after the cholera epidemic, perhaps around 1090, Lamphūn again was twice invaded and its throne usurped by unidentified raiders.

The second Lamphūn–Lop Burī war had four campaigns presumably in the decades between c. 1130–c. 1150. It again began with a Lamphūn attack on Lop Burī, led by King Āditta พระเจ้า อาทิตตราช.[3] Instead of fighting with weapons, both sides agreed to a *dhammayuddha* "a just and natural war, a righteous war"—in this case a contest in building stūpas. Lamphūn lost the contest and their army fled home. Lop Burī then retaliated three times. The first time, their army came up and engaged Lamphūn in another *dhammayuddha* war, this time excavating ponds. Now, Lamphūn won and the Lop Burī army fled. When their army came up for the second time, it was captured by Lamphūn's King Āditta while

---

3 The chronicle Jinakālamālī calls him Ditta ทิตตุ and says that he was succeeded by King Ādicca อาทิจจ. Possibly they were the same person who had a long reign, called Ādicca, Āditta in Pāli texts, and Āthit(ta) etc. in Thai texts.

it had lost its way near Lamphūn. The king had the two armies jointly build a stūpa, which he called Mahābalacetiya "Great Army Stūpa," and drink the oath water of allegiance before he released the prisoners home. Not long thereafter Lop Burī's army again was ambushed near Lamphūn but escaped. "From then on," says the chronicle Jinakālamālī, "Haripuñjaya was tranquil and in no danger."

Again, not all may be fiction because the stūpa then built is at present the principal stūpa of Wat Jām Thewī (locally called Wat Kū Kut), about 1 km west of Lamphūn. It is a large, square, pyramidal stūpa with sixty standing Buddha images in three rows on its four sides.

The Lamphūn king Āditta is also famous for another feat. Soon after his accession to the throne in about 1140–1150, a crow advised him that a Buddha relic lay buried in his garden at the place where the Buddha had once taken a meal and had predicted the future existence of Lamphūn and also the enshrinement of one of his relics by a king named Āditta. The king had his people dig for the relic. They excavated an old urn which contained an unspecified Buddha relic. He then built a pāsāda, i.e. a slender building of four pillars, open on all four sides with a tall roof, and when it was finished he placed the urn in it so that it could be viewed and the relic be worshiped from all sides. That was the beginning of the present Phra Mahā Thāt, the principal stūpa in Wat Phra Thāt Hariphunchai, one of Lān Nā's holiest stūpas. The original pāsāda was later rebuilt several times and changed into a round stūpa as it appears now. According to other traditions, the stūpa shelters a piece of bone from the skull, or three Buddha relics, viz. bone remains from the top of the head, from the chest, and from a finger. Like so many other monasteries in Lān Nā, also Wat Phra Thāt Hariphunchai goes back to a solitary *jedī* (*cetiya*) or stūpa which only much later developed into a monastery.

King Āditta's military campaign down to Lop Burī, if indeed it took place, was perhaps not entirely without result because in 1155 Lop Burī was independent enough to send an envoy to China. Then, in 1167, either the king of Lop Burī or King Āditta of Lamphūn gave the order to donate fields to the relic enshrined in a stūpa in a city then called Dhānyapura ธานยปุระ "plentiful grain city," whose remains are now known as Dong Mä Nāng Müang ดงแม่นางเมือง, located about 30 km north of Nakhòn Sawan or about 120 km north of Lop Burī. This could mean that Lop Burī was at the time either independent or under some influence from Lamphūn; perhaps the oath water of allegiance, which Āditta made the captured army from Lop Burī drink, had something to do with it.

But Lop Burī's independence did not last long. The reason why Lop Burī was able to gain temporary independence at all, probably had to do with the death of the Khmer king around 1150–1155 and some changes within Cambodia. Lamphūn may have used this transition to intervene in Lop Burī. However, after the installation of the new Khmer king, Lop Burī again fell to the Khmer and Lamphūn's influence over Lop Burī, if indeed it had had some, came to an end.

Only from c. 1200 on, did Khmer military power finally wane in central Thailand and the situation ease for Lamphūn.

Arrival of the Thais
Since c. 1050?

The first Thais reached Lān Nā from eastern and northern direc-
tions, where Thai habitats existed since of old and which still are
the homeland of many millions of Thais, namely present north
Vietnam, north Laos, south and southwest China, and northeast
Burma.[4] They came perhaps in trickles of smallish groups, during

---

4 The legendary history of the origins of the Thai, as contained in their
cosmogonies attested from Burma, Yünnan, Lān Chāng, and from the Black
Thai further east, is basically the same throughout and is similar to the one
already mentioned for Lān Nā: it differentiates between the origin of the ruling princes and the origin of the commoners. The princes came down from
heaven between c. A.D. 570 and 640 when the population was already in place;
the origin of the common people either is not explained or they had emerged
from a giant fruit such as one or more pumpkins. There are variations of the
theme, for instance the princes were hatched from eggs the size of coconuts
found in the forest (origin of the Nān dynasty).

Based on evidence from the fields of philology, ethnology, prehistory,
and physical anthropology, it has been shown that the oldest known bearers
of a Thai culture lived in c. 2000 B.C. over an extended area from (present)
Szechuan in the west towards the east, Hupei, Anhui, south Honan, south
and southeast Shantung, parts of Kiangsu; and that they are since c. 1000 B.C.
also traceable (but not necessarily newcomers) in Kwangsi, Kwangtung, south
Hunan, perhaps northeast Vietnam. An early Thai center was Hupei, and later,
Kwangsi. This has been interpreted to mean that the Chinese "high culture"
is largely based on an earlier Thai culture.

Chiefly linguistic evidence suggests that in 100 B.C.–A.D. 100 important
groups of Thai speakers lived in present southeast China / northeast Vietnam
from where, according to various kinds of evidence, some groups since c. A.D.
500–800 reached north Laos and south China and since c. 800–1050 moved
further into Laos, Thailand (occupying Khmerized Mon Sukhōthai in c.
1225–1250), northern Burma, Yünnan, and Assam.

the middle and later protohistoric period, maybe soon after the cholera epidemic of 1050, possibly even earlier. The chronicle Cāmadevīvaṃsa mentions for c. 1150 a Thai village on the Ping River near Lamphūn. The inhabitants had boats and therefore presumably were both fishermen and farmers, as so many northern Thai villages were and some still are. Basically, they were sedentary wet rice agriculturists.

The historical legends show that the autochthonous Lawa had seen the arrival of a bulk of Mon with mixed feelings. Now, about 250 years later, they witnessed the arrival of another people, the Thais. But the case of these newcomers was different. They did not come as one large group and set up two splendid cities. Rather, they seem to have come unobtrusively, and our legendary sources of the time show that their reception by the Lawa was by no means hostile, but friendly.

Some of the newly arriving Thais may have come and lived quietly by themselves (there was empty space enough for Lawa, Mon, and Thais) but others seem to have sought and received permission, even protection, from local Lawa chiefs who in their eyes were the old owners of the land. Perhaps to acknowledge an obligation, the kings of Chiang Mai, until about 1850, granted special rights and taxes to certain Lawa villages, and when in 1797, after an absence

---

The partial Thai exodus from home perhaps was caused by Imperial China's expansion along the coastal provinces southward towards Vietnam; later, by Vietnamese and Chinese pressure towards the northwest along the Red River which separated southwestern Thai groups from the rest; and by a steady growth of the Thai population, result of improved agriculture, better nutrition, and health, so that on occasion part of the population moved out.

of twenty-two years, the royal court moved back to Chiang Mai, Lawas were at the head of the ceremonial procession.

In Thai Yuan legends (for instance, The Story of Suwanna Kham Däng) the old Lawa invariably appear as a friendly, simple folk who are ruled by a chief. They live side by side with the newly arrived Yuan, and occasionally teach or inform them on local matters while the Yuan often teach them elements of Theravāda Buddhism. Sometimes the Lawa protect the Yuan from enemies, seemingly Chinese who pursue them, and save their lives. These enemies, who shoot poisoned arrows, are called spirits who come from the edge of the world, *phī khòk fā* ผีขอกฟ้า. Sometimes the Lawa king himself has to humble himself before those "spirits." Often the Lawa are guardians of religious sites, for instance places the Buddha had once visited and where he had left a head hair or a footprint. Yet, though evidently inoffensive, they are often called *milakkhu* "savages, barbarians," or even *damila*, "Tamils," which usually would be a serious charge but here only seems to mean "autochthonous people."

Near Lamphūn and Lampāng the Thais presumably lived in scattered villages close to or among the Mon, where they directly encountered Mon administration and culture. Further away to the north and east, they settled in greater numbers and under their own rulers in their own typical *bān müang* บ้านเมือง "village and country" pattern (see below).

HISTORY
c. 1200–present

The Mon Era Continued, c. 1200–1281

The Golden Age of Lamphūn
c. 1200–c. 1275

1. Overview

Lamphūn's golden time probably fell in the period between c. 1200 and c. 1275, i.e., it covered approximately the last seventy-five years of its existence as an independent city-state before the Thais captured the town. Sources reporting on this period do not so much deal with wars but rather with religious activities, donations, and construction of monastic buildings. Merit-making on such a grand scale indicates a generally peaceful time with a flourishing cultural and material life.

2. Country Affairs

King Savvādhisiddhi, c. 1200–1230
While King Āditta's reign overlaps with the end of the proto-historic and the beginning of the historic period, the city becomes

fully historical with the earliest datable stone inscriptions from 1218 and 1219. They mention activities of another of Lamphūn's famous kings, called Savvādhisiddhi สวาธิสิทธิ in his inscriptions (b. 1187), shortened to Sabbāsiddhi, in the chronicle Jinakālamālī, and in Thai writings even shorter, viz. Sapphasit สัพพสิทธิ์. He enlarged the Phra Mahā Thāt to a height of 10 m at an unknown date; in 1213 he built a monastery which he called Jetavana across the river from Lamphūn (the monastery was later called Wat Dòn by the Thais, but the site was razed in modern times and is now the school of Bān Wiang Yòng); and in 1218 he restored the big "Great Army Stūpa," damaged during an earthquake, which he called in one of his inscriptions, *Ratanacetiya* "Jewel Stūpa."

In 1219, at the age of thirty-two, he was ordained a monk in the Jetavana, with his sons Mahānama and Kaccāyana, no doubt for a limited period of time. His spiritual teacher was a *mahāthera* with the title *rājaguru* and was then eighty-two years of age, which shows that longevity at the time was not unheard of. He also built *kū* (P. *gūhā*)[1] in order to deposit holy texts in them, for instance *parittas*.[2] There still are several of such *kū* in the neighborhood of Lamphūn but their age is not certain.

Several sources report that during his lifetime monks from Sri Lanka visited Lamphūn.

---

1 *Kū* are round, stūpa- or tower-like structures. Mod. Thai คูหา "archway, cavern."

2 *Parittas* are sacred texts that protect from danger.

A possible Thai attempt to seize Lamphūn, c. 1250–1260

In about 1250–1260, when Bantoñña พันโตญญะ was king, perhaps the first attempt was made by a Thai to capture Lamphūn. One of the king's ministers or governors, whom the texts call Deyyāmacca เทยยามัจจะ, "the *āmacca* (minister) who is Thai ไทย อำมาตย์," came with an army from Lampāng, had the king killed, and seized power in Lamphūn. The sources do not mention that he became the new Lamphūn king so probably this was a short episode and the newcomer was soon replaced by another Mon king. The incident shows, however, that Thais lived among the Mon population and that one even held a powerful position in the Mon government service. It probably also shows that Lampāng then was populated and administrated by Mon.

Lamphūn fought Pagan, 1272?

The Martaban Chronicle says that in 1272 Lamphūn fought against Pagan for the ownership of Martaban. That is probably exaggerating Lamphūn's extension of power, and the event is not corroborated from other sources.

Lamphūn satellite towns

The old city of Lamphūn had satellite towns at a distance of about one day's easy journey or approximately 20 km. So far four of the towns have been identified, forming a half-circle from north through west to south: Wiang Kum Kām, Wiang Manō, Wiang Thā Kān, and Wiang Thò. The first and the third have been archeologically excavated and prepared to receive visitors.

It is unknown when they were founded and when and how they expired, but judging from finds made in them they were all active in the time of Lamphūn's glory. Wiang Thò and Wiang Manō seem to go back to about A.D. 800 and thus are perhaps nearly as old as Lamphūn; they and Wiang Kum Kām were later inhabited by Thais.

3. Everyday Life

Items of Mon material culture

One of the distinctive items of the material culture of the Lamphūn Mon was unglazed, painted pottery, and in particular water coolers with the typical long neck; they achieve the cooling effect by evaporation of some of the water through the porous wall of the container. The vessels are called *nam ton* น้ำต้น at present and are still made; glazed or in silver repoussé, they are now also used as flower vases or as decoration.

Another typical Mon item was the standing Buddha images crafted in bronze repoussé. The Mon also used to imprint or stamp scenes of the Buddha with his disciples on clay tablets, called *phra phim* พระพิมพ์ in Thai, or, on larger tablets, about five hundred tiny Buddha images sitting in rows, *phra phäng hā ròi* พระแผงห้าร้อย. The Thais later continued the tradition, especially the making of *phra phim* which are worn as amulets, but they practically abandoned the repoussé technique for making Buddha images and the stamping of *phra phäng hā ròi*, preferring instead to sculpt images from wood and to cast images in bronze.

Letters and writing

The alphabet used by the Lamphūn Mon goes back, as does
the Lop Burī Mon script, to a script used in south India. But
whereas the Lop Burī script later accepted Khmer influence, the
Lamphūn script stayed "Mon" and evolved on its own, or in conjunction with, Mon script in Burma. Though no specimens have
survived, it is hardly doubtful that the principal writing material
were specially prepared palm leaves, cut into long, narrow strips,
into which the letters were incised with a stylus. When the surface
was then smeared with a liquid containing soot and was wiped
clean, the letters clearly stood out in black from the yellowish
background of the palm leaf. The writing was "waterproof" and
the rolled documents could safely be sent away by messenger; if
rain or a wet river crossing washed the soot out, application of a
little dirt brought the writing back again. The Thais later took
over the technique. The Mon probably used the same talipat or
talipot palm, *Corypha umbraculifera*, as before them the Ceylonese
and thereafter the Thais; the latter call the tree *ton lān* ต้นลาน or
ton tān ต้นตาล, derived from tal, and therefore call the palm-leaf
writing material *bai lān* "leaf of the *lān* palm tree."

Surviving old Mon words

Various Mon words of the time survived until modern times.
The old Mon used a weight or money which, in around 1200,
the Lamphūn Mon spelled *diṅkel'* ทิงเกล์ in their inscriptions.
The word survived in the form of tical which until a few decades
ago was a common name for the official baht in Western or

Westernized merchant circles.[3] But it is curious to observe that "tical" was not used by the Yuan of northern Thailand, only by the central Thais.

The Mon counted or measured their paddy fields, which had to have low earthen dikes around them to keep the water in, by a unit spelled *bnaṅ'* พนง์ in their inscriptions. That word seems to survive in modern Thai as *phanang* ผนัง; พ(ะ)นัง "wall, dam, partition." In Lān Nā, especially, it meant "dike, embankment, levee," also "sluice, water inlet gate (for rice fields)." At present, however, the word is no longer used directly in connection with wet rice fields; the low dikes around the fields are called *khan nā* คันนา, a (central?) Thai expression.

Laws

Another interesting aspect of the spiritual culture of the Mon was their grappling with the problem of what is "appropriate and right," i.e. with laws. No doubt they had had their own traditional rules before they had become Buddhists, but through their contact with Indian culture, both Hindu and Buddhist, their perceptions underwent a change.

According to Brahmanical belief in Old India, the universe functions because of an immutable natural law, *dharma*, which in details reaches down to individuals who have to carry out

---

3 It is probable that *diṅkel'* was not a Mon word but that the Mon had learned its use from overseas merchants because the term is attested since at least 2000 B.C. in the Middle East. It is found, in slightly different forms, for instance t-q-l in Aramaic or shekel in modern Israel, from the shores of East Africa to the islands of East Indonesia (Hobson-Jobson).

appropriately their share of the *dharma*. Put otherwise, each individual, each class of people and also the king must show an appropriate behavior, *dharma*, in order not to disturb the overall *dharma* of the cosmos. General regulations and examples showed what was appropriate; people's lives should be lived according to such regulations. Very important was the *rājadharma*, the rules of which governed the behavior proper for a king.

The more practical aspects of the *dharma*, for example, the appropriate actions for carrying out rites, sacrifices, purifications, administration of justice, etc., were written down from c. 500 B.C. in books called *dharmasūtra* "dharma text book," then in books called *dharmaśāstra* "the science of dharma." The best known is the Mānavadharmaśāstra มานวธรรมศาสตร์, also called Manusmṛti มนุสมฤติ (มนุศาร), composed perhaps between 200 B.C. and A.D. 200; according to legend it was miraculously revealed to a seer or sage called Manu.

Therefore, a ruler in Old India did not create laws. He decided individual cases following the spirit of the *dharma* as found in the *dharmaśāstra* books. But one king's or judge's decision was not a binding precedent for other rulers or judges.

The Mon around Pegu-Martaban accepted and absorbed, with other Indian ideas, the general line of the *dharma* concept but, being Theravāda Buddhists, removed the purely Brahmanical parts. They kept the concept of an overall world law and the necessity to follow it, and also the sections on the administration of justice, then added a few local customary rules, and so came to compose their own *dharmaśāstra* books that they called, since they wrote in Pāli and not in Sanskrit, *dhammasattha*. They produced a great many of them between c. 1000 and 1300. One of them was compiled c. 1290 on the initiative of King Wārerū วาเรรู (Jao Fā Rua เจ้าฟ้ารัว[4]) of Martaban, who, according to the legend, was married to a daughter of King Rām Khamhäng of Sukhōthai. This Wārerū version was famous through the ages not only in Burma; traces of it can still be seen in the introductory *dhammasattha* of the Bangkok law codex of 1805, *Kotmāi Trā Sām Duang* กฎหมาย ตราสามดวง "Law Book with the Three Seals."

While the *dhammasatthas* treated justice matters more in general, the Mon of Burma also invented "real" law cases, often based on Jātaka stories.[5] Collections of such imaginary cases were called *rājasatthas* "the science of kings."

Since the Mon in Pegu wrote *dhammasatthas* and *rājasatthas*, the Mon in Lamphūn surely were acquainted with them and presumably also composed a few of their own and emended existing ones, though none seem to have survived. How much these works were indeed applied to decide cases in everyday life is unknown. One is tempted to speculate that their "everyday laws" were a mixture of their own old traditions with these newer *dhammasatthas* and *rājasatthas*. These, in turn, later had a profound influence on the laws of the Thais of Lān Nā.

---

4 In Western literature, also called Mogado, Makatho, Wagaru.

5 Jātakas are stories about the previous lives of the Buddha.

The Thais Consolidate
c. 1260–1281

1. Overview

While the Mon of Lamphūn and Lampāng led a peaceful and probably quite wealthy life, their immediate northern neighbors, the Thais, presumably felt the repercussions of the dynastic change in China. Within four years, between 1253 and 1257, Kublai Khan and his Mongol-Chinese armies had subjected the once powerful Dali (Tali) kingdom, the Thai Lü kingdom of Chiang Rung in Sip-sòng Phan Nā (Xishuangbanna), and then all of Yünnan. In 1258 his armies arrived in Tongking.

With Muslim traders, who settled along the trade routes and married local women, and with the Mongol armies, largely composed of Turk ("Taruk") groups, Islam came to Yünnan. The first governor whom Kublai Khan nominated in Yünnan was a Muslim, Omar from Buchara in Uzbekistan. He and many others were probably Hui Muslims. This particular group of Muslims was centered in present northwest China and beyond, Sinkiang (Tarim), Alma Ater, Uzbekistan. It seems likely that their name Hui was the origin of the generic name Hò ฮ่อ (in Thai Yuan texts usually ห้อ, หร้อ) which the Thai used (and still use) to call the Chinese Yünnan Muslims, often in particular the people from Dali.[6]

---

6 The modern appellation is Jīn Hò จีนฮ่อ "Hò - Chinese," i.e. a person from China who is not a "real" Chinese but a Hò. In the nineteenth century also, various bands of robbers emanating from southern China were indiscriminately called Hò, whether they were genuine Hò or not.

In 1260 Kublai Khan overthrew the Chinese Sung dynasty and became the first emperor of the new Mongol-Chinese Yüan dynasty.

In 1267 the fifth son of the emperor was nominated "Prince of Yünnan" and came to reside in Dali. The rank of the emperor's representatives seems to have oscillated between a high "viceroy" (in Kunming) and a relatively low "governor" (in Dali) but it is clear that these officials dealt, in the name of the emperor, with the outlying foreign countries. As the Yüan did with other countries, so was Viceroy Nasr-uddin instructed to demand tokens of submission from Pagan in 1271, and again in 1273. The Burmese king then murdered the entire second Chinese mission and thus precipitated a number of Chinese retaliatory campaigns, the first in 1277, and then in 1287 Pagan fell to the Mongols.

The various little Thai states, *müang* เมือง, to the south of Yünnan, certainly followed these events with a good deal of awe. The Thai Yuan in the Lān Nā area consolidated their position by expanding into hitherto unsettled places and also by seizing smaller Thai city-states near them and adding them to their kingdom.

2. Country Affairs

The main group of Thais that came to settle in Lān Nā was called by its neighbors Yuan, Yūn or Yōn, (Yonaka in Pāli texts, re-Thai-ized as Yōnok). The Yuan lived in the region where the three countries of Burma, Laos, and Thailand now meet, or somewhat further north; later text sources written in Pāli call the land Yonaraṭṭha โยนรฏฐ "the Yuan State."

Their first known, fully historical ruler, was Phayā Mang Rāi พญามังราย; the name means literally "King Prince Rāi." He was the twenty-fifth king of the Lāo dynasty founded by the mythical Lāo Jong who was believed to have descended stairs down from heaven to rule over a populated country that lacked a king. Mang Rāi (born c. 1239) was the son of Lāo Meng who ruled over a little kingdom, Müang Rāo or Müang Lāo, also called Müang Ngön Yāng / Yāng Ngön, located seemingly in the general area of present Mä Sāi - Chiang Sän. His mother, Lāo Meng's queen, was a daughter of the king of Chiang Rung[7] and therefore a Thai Lü.

The Lü were, and still are, a major Thai group in present southwest Yünnan, China. Their capital, Chiang Rung on the Mä Khòng River was founded in 1180 and is located about 200 km to the north-northeast of Chiang Sän. At the time it was the most important of the city-states in the region called until today, Sip-sòng Phan Nā[8] "Twelve Districts."

In 1261, upon the death of his father, Mang Rāi became king of the Yuan in Müang Rāo at the age of twenty-two.

At the time there was yet another Thai kingdom, Phayao, located about 150 km to the southwest of Mang Rāi's realm. Its first king is said to have been the second son of a king of the Lāo Jong dynasty who could not become ruler in Müang Rāo. The young prince was therefore sent forth, well equipped with personnel and animals by his royal father, to occupy and rule the Phayao

---

7 Local Thai pronunciation: Jiang Hung; Chinese: Jinghong, formerly also Cheli, Chöli.

8 Local Lü pronunciation: Sip-sòng Phan Nā; Chinese: Xishuangbanna.

country. Legendary histories unanimously name this first Phayao ruler, Phayā or Khun Jòm Tham or Jòm Phā Rüang, but variously date the founding of Phayao to between about 1090 and 1150.

Mang Rāi's possessions initially included only Fāng to the west and Chiang Kham to the south of the Chiang Sän area. He soon began to enlarge his kingdom and influence towards the south. In 1263 he founded Chiang Rāi "King Mang Rāi's City" which became his capital, taking a little hill by the Mä Kok River, Dòi Tòng, as the spiritual center of his country (*sadü müang* สะดือเมือง). Then he proceeded to subdue some settlements already in Thai hands such as Chiang Khòng in 1269.

The chronicles give two reasons for Mang Rāi's expansionism. First, as a direct descendant of Lāo Jong, as the senior of the line invested with the sword, the knife, and certain jewelry attesting to his rightful consecration as king, he felt insufficiently honored by other rulers nearby who, though also descended from Lāo Jong, belonged to lesser lines and had not been consecrated; second, the population of Müang Rāo / Müang Ngön Yāng increased so much that living space became insufficient. Evidently he saw no opportunities in the north, east, or west, presumably because here all space was already occupied, as with the Thai Lü in Sip-sòng Phan Nā. In particular the north was an area from which pressure emanated southwards towards Lān Nā: Mongol China was trying to push beyond Yünnan towards mainland Southeast Asia. The Mongol Yüan dynasty at the time was expanding not only into Yünnan but also into Burma and Tongking.

In the face of these developments it appears that Mang Rāi had a policy of consolidating Thai power in the region next to him as much as possible under his own rule.

3. Everyday Life

The Thai Yuan, one of many Thai groups, were not illiterate when they arrived in Lān Nā. They were not unfamiliar with Buddhism either, and their administrative and social organization, together with their material and technical civilization, was more refined, advanced, and effective than those of the local Lawa and Khā tribes. They had mastered the art of administrating a larger area from one central settlement under the leadership of a prince by sending their children forth to new lands and keeping some paternal authority over them and their land.

The Yuan basically were farmers with both horticulture and agriculture. Their staple food was the sticky glutinous rice, *khao nüng* เข้านึ่ง "steamed rice,"[9] that was grown on wet rice or paddy fields *nā* นา and that was steamed instead of boiled for consumption. They had upland gardens, *rai* ไร่, where they grew vegetables and other crops; and they also did some hunting and fishing and

---

9 Many northern Thai groups, such as the Yuan, the Khün, the Lü, pronounce the word for rice with a short *a*, *khao* เข้า, not as in modern central Thai, with a long *ā*, *khāo* ข้าว.

As is evident from remains in straw-fired bricks, it seems that all archaic Thai groups grew glutinous rice but that those groups who settled in central Thailand later switched to non-glutinous rice, perhaps under the influence of Khmer or Mon eating habits.

collected forest products such as honey. But among them were also craftsmen who produced simple technical objects such as pottery and metal items, and there were local as well as foreign merchants who effectively traded over greater distances. Presumably, much as was the case in later times, some villages had their specialties but on the whole the occupations of the villagers were not monotonously uniform.

The nucleus of their society was the family, and in many important matters the family put the emphasis on women. The family was matrilocal, i.e. the young husband went to live with his wife and her parents, at least for a short time.

The family spirits, or ancestor spirits, *phī pū yā* ผีปู่ย่า, were "handed down" in the female line, usually from mother to eldest daughter. The senior woman occupied the family's house, which had the spirit shrine; her house was the *hüan kao* เฮือนเก๊า (เรือนเค้า), the "stem house," and she was the chief officiant of the family spirits.

Descent was usually counted in the female line (X is the son/ daughter of Mrs. Y, not of Mr. Z), but sometimes in the male line; the latter perhaps especially often in the "higher society" or aristocracy. Male children were often named according to birth order, their number being their personal name, or part of their name. The custom continued for a long time; famous King Tilōka Rāt (Tilokarāja) was at birth Thāo Lok ท้าวลก, i.e. the sixth royal prince, "Prince Sextus."

In their spiritual culture they appear to have been sophisticated animists. If present traditions (recorded from among the non-Buddhist Thai of north Vietnam and north Laos, and the Buddhist Yuan of Lān Nā in the nineteenth and twentieth centuries) are an indication, they thought that natural phenomena had souls, that certain objects, such as trees and even persons, were animated or inhabited by spirits, and they also believed in the existence of a set of souls in the human body.

They believed in a couple of divine givers of life called *Thän* แถน a woman and a man who live somewhere inaccessible and take the life-essence from their own body parts, from their hand, foot, chest, etc., out of which the new child is born and grows (a variant of the so-called Hainuwele motif, well known among archaic agriculturist groups, for instance, in the eastern Indonesian islands). They also believed in some kind of life after death: they erected little huts over the graves of their dead in which they placed all kinds of provisions for the deceased. They performed ancestor worship honoring the mostly benevolent ancestor spirits, *phī pū yā*, who were transmitted in the female line as already mentioned, and also honored the spirits of former owners of local plots of land, *jao thī* เจ้าที่. Besides, they believed in non-specific forest and tree spirits, *phī pā* ผีป่า. In particular the simple populace probably viewed Buddhism as another form of spirit service. Important decisions were made by consulting chicken bones.

We do not know very much about their material culture, but one can suppose that the Thais arriving here clothed themselves in cotton fabric and surely knew silk. The women presumably adorned their clothing with patterns that originally had a likeness to patterns of the Dong Son culture in north Vietnam and beyond, as found for instance on old Dong Son bronze kettle drums, but the farther they traveled west and the longer they were separated from their old homes, the old patterns lost their distinctiveness, and new designs were added. A similar development took place in the other aspects of their life—language, physical appearances, tools, etc.—through intermixture with locals.

Their villages seem to have been open settlements but they stockaded or otherwise fortified important places. A village usually had a *jai bān* ใจบ้าน "community pillar" as its spiritual center, i.e. one or several pillars of modest size arranged as a group. Larger settlements had a *sao sadü müang* เสาสะดือเมือง or *lak müang* หลักเมือง, a tall "city navel pillar" or "country post," sometimes also more than one. Later, Chiang Mai was to have something similar, presumably gleaned from Hindu India: a prosperity-bringing, danger-dispelling *sao Inta khīn*, Indakhīla, "Indra's pillar." Its remains are thought to be embedded beneath a brick altar standing in a separate pavilion in Wat Jedī Luang.

The Quick End of the Mon Era
c. 1275–1281

King Yībā was the last Mon king of Lamphūn. It seems that during his time the city-state was highly prosperous, and that this very prosperity both attracted the Thais and caused him to become negligent in his personal supervision of the country's administration. That led to the capture of the city by Mang Rāi and to his departure.

In about 1274 Phayā Mang Rāi learned from traders of the prosperity of Lamphūn (Hariphunchai) and wished to capture the city-state for himself, but he and his councilors thought that their army was not strong enough for a direct attack. Mang Rāi therefore decided on a stratagem. He dismissed for an alleged grave offense his minister of records, Āi Fā, and the latter sought refuge and employ with King Yība in Lamphūn. He soon obtained the king's approval to screen all matters presented to the king and to handle practically everything himself. He thus isolated the king from the population and then committed outrageous misdeeds in the name of the king, such as dragging timber for the construction of the king's new palace through newly planted rice fields. When people complained, he claimed to obey only orders, and used the occasion to add that Mang Rāi would never have given such orders. The population became malcontent with King Yība and when, after six to seven years, the people were sufficiently exasperated, Mang Rāi arrived with his army. The people gladly received him and Yība fled to Lampāng, which was ruled by his son, Phayā Bök. Mang Rāi thus seized one of the major kingdoms of the region without bloodshed in 1281.[10] The Chiang Mai Chronicle says that he ceremoniously took his seat on the throne of Lamphūn on Wednesday, 23 April 1281, at the hour Kòng Ngāi, i.e. between 7:30 and 9:00 a.m. He was then forty-three years old.

Thus ended the Mon political supremacy in this part of the north. Though the royal family left, the mass of the Mon population with its monk-scholars and artisans stayed on and became the teachers of the Thais in many fields.

---

10 It is curious that one of the major northern chronicles, the Jinakālamālī, dates the event to 1292.

Minister Āi Fā is not only remembered for his ruse in the capture of Lamphūn. In about 1277–1280 he also dug a long, important irrigation canal, using water from the Mä Ping River. It began about 35 km north of Chiang Mai on the left bank of the Ping, about 1.5 km upstream from the mouth of the Mä Täng แม่แตง, then ran along the foot of the hills first south and then east, to join after about 36 km the Mä Kuang แม่กวง near present Bān Müang Wa บ้านเมืองวะ, about 6 km west of Amphö Dòi Saket. It opened up and irrigated fields in the northeast of Lamphūn. Thousands of people worked on its excavation. Since much of the work was done during the hot season when the earth is as hard as rock or, as the Chiang Mai Chronicle puts it, "when one digs into the soil and sparks fly" ขุดดินเป็นไฟออก (the choice of season being another deliberate bullying action on the part of the minister), the canal was dubbed *müang kheng* เหมืองแข็ง "hard canal." Parts of it can still be seen today, called "the old Mä Fäk Canal" เหมืองแม่แฝกเก่า,[11] also *müang khī nī* เหมืองขี้หนี้, which is understood as "canal of unkept promises." When in modern times the Irrigation Department sought to improve and regulate irrigation in the area, a new Mä Fäk Canal was dug not far from and along the general lines of the old one.

---

11 The little brook Mä Fäk joins the canal around the midpoint of its course.

The Thai Era of Lān Nā, 1281–present

The Making of Lān Nā
1281–1371

1. Overview

With the acquisition of Lamphūn in 1281, the nucleus of the political entity "Lān Nā" had been created. It consisted of two main parts, a southern and a northern part, or, as the historian Ratanapañña called them in his chronicle Jinakālamālī (1517), the Yonaraṭṭha โยนรฏฐ and the Biṅgaraṭṭha พิครฏฐ, i.e. the Yuan state and the Ping state.

Lān Nā now went through a formative period during which her new masters acquired the remaining territory in between, namely Lampāng and Phayao; founded a new capital city in the southern part, Chiang Mai; and administratively united all parts. That period of making Lān Nā ended when the diverse Mon and Thai items of spiritual and material culture had been organized and "digested." Thus, Lān Nā's initial political and geographical period ended in about 1340–1350 still without Nān and Phrä, and her period of adaptation and learning ended in the years after 1360 when she began to be creative on her own. The years 1369–1371, when a monk introduced new values from the outside, may serve as a cut-off date.

2. Country Affairs

Connections with Pegu and Pagan, c. 1290?

The Chiang Mai Chronicle reports that Mang Rāi, after his conquest of Lamphūn (1281), went to "visit" two important kingdoms in the southwest and west.

While still living in Kum Kām (1286–1296, see below) Mang Rāi went with his army to the borders of Pegu (Hongsāwadī หงสาวดี, Haṃsavati หํสวติ), asked for presents, and closed an alliance with the local Mon king who gave him his daughter in marriage. The chronicle calls her Nāng Phaikō นางพายโค "Lady Pegu นางพะโค." The king here would have been Wārerū, the well-known initiator of the Wārerū *dhammasattha* and supposed son-in-law of the Sukhōthai king Rām Khamhäng whose daughter he had married.

Some time later Mang Rāi went to the borders of "Müang PūKām Angwa," i.e. Pagan-Ava, where he asked the king for, and obtained, a number of skilled metal craftsmen, notably bronze, gold, silver, and iron smiths. The bronze smiths were settled at Chiang Sän, the goldsmiths in Chiang Tung and the others in Wiang Kum Kām.

How much historical truth these accounts contain is unknown; they are not confirmed by Mon or Burmese sources. In particular the Ava-Pegu episode is problematic. Ava was founded only in 1364, Chiang Sän only in 1327, both after his death. Perhaps these two accounts are garbled accounts of events that were actually somewhat different.

The foundation of Chiang Mai, 1296

Mang Rāi evidently did not wish to live in Lamphūn though from now on he preferred the new southern part of his kingdom and did not go back to Chiang Rāi. In 1283, he made Āi Fā governor of Lamphūn and moved on to found a new town.

During several years he tried out or inspected sites for his new capital city. In total, he built one new site, rebuilt an old town, and inspected five more places before he was satisfied with the seventh locality, the future Chiang Mai. The site he newly built up, complete with a specially dug water channel and boat landing, was Chiang Lö เชียงเลอ. It probably was located northeast of Lamphūn but its exact location is unknown. However, this site turned out to be prone to flooding, was a complete failure, and had to be abandoned. The old town he rebuilt and lived in from 1286 was Wiang Kum Kām, an old Mon satellite town of Lamphūn, 4 km southeast of present Chiang Mai. He was not fully satisfied with it, either, and kept looking for better places.

Finally in 1292, while hunting on the west bank of the Mä Ping, not far from the hill Dòi Suthep, he discovered a very suitable place with a good omen. On the Thai New Year's Day, Thursday, 27 March 1292, he ceremoniously went to live there but did not yet officially found the city. Four years later he founded Chiang Mai "New Town" here, on Thursday, 12 April 1296. Present were his two royal friends, Phayā Ruang (also called King Rām or Rām Khamhäng) of Sukhōthai and Phayā Ngam Müang of Phayao with whom he had consulted on the size of the new capital, appr. 1.7 x 1.5 km (at present a square of 1.5 x 1.5 km). The Three Kings Monument in Chiang Mai (1984) shows the three princes deliberating.

From then on Chiang Mai was the capital city of Lān Nā except during the period 1311–1339 (or 1345) when first Chiang Rāi and then newly built Chiang Sän, were the capitals. During that time, the Lān Nā king or overlord resided in Chiang Rāi or Chiang Sän, while one of his sons ruled Chiang Mai as the father's vassal, becoming overlord himself and moving up to Chiang Rāi or Chiang Sän upon the death of his father.

The acquisition of Lampāng, 1296

As has been told above, when Mang Rāi seized Lamphūn in 1281, King Yībā of Lamphūn fled to Lampāng where his son Bök was king. Fifteen years later, in the same year in which Mang Rāi founded Chiang Mai, 1296, the Yuan defeated the Lampāng Mon in a great battle. King Bök was killed, the Yuan seized Lampāng, and ex-king Yībā fled south to Phitsanulōk.

The Yuan now, viz. in about 1300, controlled approximately the western half of Lān Nā. Still outside their reach was Phayao in the center, and Pua / Nān and Phrä in the east.

The possession of Chiang Mai, Lamphūn, and Lampāng meant for them easier access to Sukhōthai, Lop Burī, later also to Ayuthayā (founded in 1351), and to Moulmein, Martaban, Pegu, i.e. to the Gulf of Siam and to the Indian Ocean.

From now on the Chiang Mai - Lamphūn region became known as *Pingkha Rattha* พิงครัฏฐะ "the (River) Ping State" (P. Bingaraṭṭha) to distinguish it from the old northern part of the kingdom, the *Yōna Rattha* โยนรัฏฐะ "Yuan State" (P. Yonaraṭṭha).

China expands southward

Mang Rāi's effort to unite power in his hand perhaps was not just a personal ambition for conquest but also had political reasons. China under the Mongol Yüan emperors was expanding towards the south, as has been said above. Between 1253 and 1257 China subjected all of Yünnan including Dali and the Sip-sòng Phan Nā with Chiang Rung, his mother's home; in 1258 it invaded Tongking; in 1287 Chinese forces seized Pagan.

In that year, 1287, Mang Rāi and the rulers of Phayao (Ngam Müang) and Sukhōthai (Rām Khamhäng or Ruang) concluded a pact of friendship at Phayao. According to the Chiang Mai Chronicle he reconciled the other two princes who had a personal quarrel. But he may also have acted to avoid disunity among important Thai groups in the face of the Chinese advance. Whatever the background of that pact, Mang Rāi obviously was one of three powerful Thai leaders of his time, and all three were on friendly terms.

In 1296, the year in which Chiang Mai was founded and Lampāng seized by the Thais, the Chinese fully incorporated Chiang Rung with the Sip-sòng Phan Nā into their administrative bureaucracy as the Chinese province of Chö-li.

From then on there were intermittent struggles between Thais, Chinese, and later Burmese, for the general area of Chiang Rung - Chiang Tung - Chiang Rāi. This unsettled state of affairs ended only at the end of the nineteenth century when it was finally agreed that Chiang Rung was to be under China, Chiang Tung under Burma, and Chiang Rāi under Siam (Thailand).

It is therefore probable that during the decades of Mongol China's expansion towards the south, between approximately 1260 and 1310, Lān Nā began to send presents or tribute to Yünnan in order to cultivate friendly relations and to avoid being seized as had happened to the Sip Sòng Phan Nā with Chiang Rung. Also the powerful Thai state of Sän Wī next to Yünnan had to stay on good terms with China.[12]

On the other hand, in 1299, Thai Yuan soldiers may have gone to assist Müang Kyaukse, a Buddhist Shan State,[13] which was opposing the king of Pagan because the latter had, forcibly, become a friend and supporter of the Mongol-Chinese.

Mang Rāi's Lān Nā was far enough from the Chinese empire that it did not have to fight directly against her invading armies. It is sometimes said that Chiang Mai, or northern Lān Nā, was also attacked by the Chinese who called it *Pa-peh (pai)* or *Pa-peh (pai)-si-fu* "Eight hundred wives." But the Chinese sources perhaps meant some other township that existed already before Chiang Mai and that was culturally different because they say, for instance, that already in 1292 (i.e. four years before the foundation of Chiang Mai) the emperor called for an attack on the *Pa-pai-hsi-fu* kingdom and that traditionally this tribal chieftain had eight hundred wives, each controlling one stockade. That does not sound like a Thai or Mon state.

---

12 The state seal used by the *jao fā* (lord) of Sän Wī until 1890 was an old Chinese seal issued in 1371 reading in Chinese, "Seal of the hereditary chieftain of Muh Pang," the Chinese name for Sän Wī.

13 Shan is a Western and Burmese appellation for the various Thai groups in Burma, sometimes also used for those in China and Assam.

The extent of Mang Rāi's Lān Nā

Phayā Mang Rāi died in 1311 or 1317. The Chiang Mai Chronicle says he was struck by lightning in the center of Chiang Mai. According to local belief, he became a guardian spirit of the country.

At the time of his death, the northern border of his kingdom probably was north of Mä Sāi, somewhere between Müang Nāi - Müang Phān เมืองพาน and Chiang Tung, perhaps even including Chiang Tung; the southern border was between Lampāng and Uttaradit - Tāk; the eastern border was at the Mä Khòng near the future Chiang Sän; and the western border was somewhere between Chiang Mai and the Salween River. Phayao and Phrä were not yet included, nor was Pua, and Nān had not yet been founded.

Thus, at the beginning, the polity Lān Nā covered about five to six provinces of present north Thailand plus perhaps a part of present east Burma, south of or up to Chiang Tung. The whole was more or less united as one country, or at least the various rather independent city-states recognized Phayā Mang Rāi as their overlord. For that reason one can consider Phayā Mang Rāi as the founder of Lān Nā. But it is unknown whether the term Lān Nā was already used in his time.

Chiang Rāi and Chiang Sän as capitals, 1318–1345 or 1311–1339

Mang Rāi had let his son, Khun Khrām (Mang Khrām, Chai Songkhrām), rule in Chiang Rāi. After his death, Chai Songkhrām became the overlord. He installed his eldest son, Sän Phū, in Chiang Mai and continued to live in Chiang Rāi, which was now the site of the main court and therefore Lān Nā's capital city.

Our historical sources are not in agreement about what happened next. It seems that Sän Phū soon was ousted from Chiang Mai by the ruler of Müang Nāi (Moné, in the Shan States) who was his father's younger brother and therefore his uncle, called Khun Khrüa. Sän Phū fled to his father in Chiang Rāi. Thereupon his father Chai Songkhrām had his other son, Nam Thuam of Fāng, remove Khrüa from Chiang Mai and installed Nam Thuam as ruler instead. He later exiled Nam Thuam to Chiang Tung and had Sän Phū return to Chiang Mai for a second time. Whatever the factual happenings, they show that Chiang Mai was a very desirable city-state to rule, and that then, as in the future, the regular succession of rulership was from father to (eldest) son, not to his brother.

After the death of Chai Songkhrām in 1325 (or 1327), Sän Phū became the overlord. He installed his son Kham Fū in Chiang Mai and moved up to Chiang Rāi.

In 1325 he founded a town at the confluence of the Mä Kok and the Mä Khōng. This town is called Chiang Sän Nòi "Little Chiang Sän" in western travel literature of the nineteenth century, and Wiang Prüksā เวียงปรึกษา "Consult-Town" in legends and myth-chronicles. It is located 4–5 km southeast of present Chiang Sän. Much of its ruined earth walls and monasteries can still be seen. The Mä Kok River is now about 1.5 km further east but aerial photographs show that formerly the town was directly on the north bank of a loop of the winding river, in the north flanked by the Mä Khōng and in the south and southeast by the Mä Kok.

In 1327 he founded another town a few kilometers upriver, on the right or western bank of the Mä Khōng. This town bears his name, Chiang Sän "City of (King) Sän (Phū)." He went to live there and Chiang Sän became his new capital.

Chiang Mai became the capital again under Phayā Phā Yū, in 1339 or 1345.

Phayao is joined to Lān Nā, 1338

Sän Phū's son and successor, Phayā Kham Fū, in 1338 annexed the principality of Phayao with the help of the independent ruler of Pua, the predecessor town of Nān.

Thus, by around 1340, most of Lān Nā (north, west, center, and much of the south) was ruled by the Yuan and was directly or indirectly controlled or influenced by Chiang Mai. Within a relatively short time, about sixty years, the Yuan had replaced the Mon as the region's administrators on a state level and now controlled a wider area than the Lamphūn - Lampāng Mon had done.

Pua, Phrä, and Nān remain outside Lān Nā

The incorporation of Pua, Nān, and Phrä into the Lān Nā conglomerate did not succeed for another hundred years because they had a strong relationship with Sukhōthai, sometimes as vassals and sometimes as independent allies. Only after Sukhōthai had lost her power to Ayuthayā could these city-states be joined to Lān Nā under Chiang Mai supremacy.

Here, protohistory and history began later than in western and central Lān Nā. In about 1250, the region of the uppermost Nān and Yom Rivers were settled by a group of people called the *Kāo* or *Kwāo* กาว, กวาว, among others, in some texts pali-ized as Kāva. They are mentioned several times in our sources but their ethnic-

ity, Thai or otherwise, is not known. Their first king, according
to the legend, was Khun Fòng ขุนฟอง "Prince Egg," hatched from
an egg the size of a coconut that had been found in the forest by
a hunter. The prince was brought up at the court of Phayā Phū
Khā who ruled M. Yāng (which obviously was located in that
area and whose people were of an unknown race). When Khun
Fòng reached the age of sixteen, the king gave him permission to
have his own kingdom. A hermit traced the outline of the type
Tejaka bayuha เตชะกะพะยุหะ for the capital city with his walking
staff on the ground. The town was therefore called Wòra Nakhòn
(P. Varanagara), but the people later called it Müang Pua (at
present the old ruined city at Amphö Pua, about 50 km north
of Nān, not far from the Nān River). A local population lived
there already, Kāo people, and Khun Fòng became their king,[14]
perhaps in about 1240–1260.

Later, in the decades around 1300, suzerainty over the region
was contested. Already Mang Rāi tried to extend his power into
that region. Still ruling from Chiang Rāi, he fought with an
unnamed Kāo king in 1274 and took from him the town Dada-
rapura. The town has not yet been identified but seems to have
been near Phrä. It appears in the chronicle Jinakālamālī until after
1500 and possibly in a Phrä inscription of 1529 under the name
of M. Tāt เมืองตาด.

Mang Rāi's success was either only partial or short-lived because
between c. 1280 and 1300, i.e. in the time of Rām Khamhäng,

---

14 Another egg, found by the hunter on the same occasion, hatched first;
that prince became the first ruler of Wiang Jan (Vientiane) in Laos.

Pua and Phrä were under Sukhōthai, at least nominally, according to the controversial inscription no.1, the "Rām Khamhäng inscription."

Only a few years later (c. 1310?), King Ngam Müang of then still independent Phayao seized Pua. He installed one of his queens as regent and Pua now nominally was under Phayao. However, Ngam Müang and his queen had a quarrel over a dish of curry, and she then married the grandson of Khun Fòng, Phä Nòng, who became king of Pua in c. 1322. So the city-state reverted to the Pua dynasty. He is counted as the third king of the Pua - Nan dynasty.

While details and dates before c. 1322 are shaky, it is certain that from then on Pua and Phrä were virtually independent for a while though amicably allied with Sukhōthai.

Between 1325 and 1334, during the time of Phayā Sän Phū, his son, the future Phayā Kham Fū, fought the Kāo king, or a Kāo king, and captured Müang Phrä. That Kāo king could have been Phä Nòng, ruler of Pua, but it is unknown if at the time he also ruled over Phrä.

In 1338 the Kāo ruler of Pua, Phä Nòng, assisted Phayā Kham Fū, ruling from Chiang Sän, to seize Phayao, which had been independent until then. The two princes then quarreled over the booty, Phä Nòng went to plunder Fāng, their armies fought, and Kham Fū defeated Phä Nòng who withdrew to Pua.

A new effort by Chiang Mai to advance into that region was made in 1340 when King Kham Fū, who had earlier taken Phrä but obviously could not hold on to it, tried to seize the city but was not successful.

In about 1358 Phayā Kān Müang of Pua built the famous stūpa Phra Thāt Chä Häng, about 50 km south of Pua close to the east bank of the Nān River, in order to enshrine relics and votive tablets. He had received them from the king of Sukhōthai because he had gone and helped him with the construction of a monastery in Sukhōthai.[15] In 1359 he left Pua and moved his court to a new town, Chä Häng, built at the stūpa. The Kāo people, says the Nān Chronicle, came to help with the construction of the royal palace, which sounds as if his own people were not Kāo, perhaps Thai.

But already in 1368, because of a shortage of water there, his successor Phā Kòng moved to the other side of the river where he founded his new capital city, Nān, on the present site of the town.

Those were politically difficult times for Sukhōthai and Nān -Phrä but they were able to preserve their independence for decades because they assisted each other on occasion. Sukhōthai was under pressure from Ayuthayā (founded in 1351), and was in particular the object of attacks from the Suphan Burī faction, one of the two factions fighting for the Ayuthayā throne. Nān was not spared; two of her kings may have been killed by Suphan Burī agents, in 1363 and 1398. Sukhōthai's army helped with local difficulties

---

15 In the Nān chronicles, between 1353–1600, there is usually a discrepancy of two years between the name and the number of a year, viz. the name is two years ahead of the number. The reason for that is not clear. Many authors, including Griswold/Prasöt and Wyatt, accept the names as correct; I have reasons to prefer the numbers as correct. Therefore, my dates may be later by two years than theirs, if based on a Nān chronicle in that period.

in Phrä (1359–1360; Phayā Lüthai stayed for seven months in Phrä) and in Nān (c. 1362; Phayā Lüthai himself led the army).

The end of the tribute to the Hò / China, c. 1370

It is unknown exactly when and under which circumstances the Yuan began to send tribute, *suai* ส่วย, to Yünnan. It presumably happened after about 1260, under Chinese-Mongol pressure through the governor or viceroy in Yünnan. Thai Yuan texts call this official respectfully *Phayā Hò, Jao Lum Fā* พญาฮ่อเจ้าลุ่มฟ้า "the Hò lord, prince under the sky," and occasionally add two more words which are not well understood, viz. *Pao Phimān* เปา (or เพา) ภิมาน. Obviously the tribute was paid to Yünnan, not to Peking or the central government in China; the word "China" does not occur at all.

The Chiang Mai Chronicle claims that in the time of Phayā Kü Nā (1367–1388 or 1355–1385) the paying of tribute to the Hò lord ended. The tribute, says the chronicle, consisted of nine thousand double baskets of rice,[16] which the Hò came to fetch themselves. The end of tribute paying presumably had to do with the end of the Mongol Yüan dynasty in 1368. The subsequent Ming dynasty later tried in vain to revive the tribute.

While it seems plausible that with the end of the pressure from the Mongol-Chinese Yuan dynasty came an end in tribute paying, the quantity and the kind of tribute allegedly demanded raise questions. The amount of rice, nine thousand double baskets carried by one person on a pole, *kān / khān* คาน, seems far too high. Interesting is the kind of rice specified. It is not the glutinous rice the Yuan usually

---

16 The text has /สวยเขาเชา 9 พันคาน / i.e. ส่วยข้าวเจ้า 9,000 คาน.

eat but specifically *khao jao*, non-glutinous rice, which the Chinese eat. That rice was in the more recent past, if at all, planted by the Yuan as a second crop for trading with the outside. It would mean that either already before 1300 Lān Nā planted two rice crops, or else the ruler imported rice from the outside for the tribute.

3. Everyday Life

Continued importance of Lamphūn

With Mang Rāi's conquest of Lamphūn and the departure of the Mon court, the city's political power ended. But the mass of its population stayed on and continued to be of importance in spiritual and material matters. When Phayā Lü Thai of Sī Sachanālai (the future king Mahādhammarāja I of Sukhōthai) in 1345 wrote his famous treatise on Buddhist cosmogony and cosmology, *Traibhūmikathā,* now usually known as *Traiphūm Phra Ruang* "The Three Worlds according to Phra Ruang," he had previously consulted per messenger also with Mahāthera Buddhaghosācāriya of Lamphūn.

The Yuan kings acknowledged the spiritual importance of Lamphūn; between c. 1325 and 1345 the Phra Mahā Thāt, still only a stūpa without surrounding monastery, was built over and embellished with eight over-life-size bronze repoussé Buddha images that were fastened around the bell-shaped upper section (*aṇḍa, khò rakhang* คอระฆัง). Though they were thickly covered with protective coating and gilding in the last restoration in 1980, they are still faintly visible from below, in particular when the sun is in the right position early in the morning or in late afternoon.

The Lamphūn pottery kilns not only kept up their production but even developed their wares further.

Above all, the Yuan learned from the Lamphūn Mon certain finer points. When they first arrived in Lān Nā, the Yuan were neither illiterate nor unfamiliar with Buddhism, and their administrative and social organization, together with their material and technical civilization, was more refined, advanced, and effective than those of local tribes. But their culture had not yet fully reached the stage which ethnologists call Hochkultur "high culture," i.e. an advanced spiritual culture founded on abstract principles and written authority, based on an administration that incorporates more than only neighboring villages, and accompanied by a major material culture able to create, for instance, important buildings or other technical items.

It seems that the Yuan's living side by side with the Buddhist Lamphūn Mon was the impetus that advanced them to a "high culture." By about 1350–1375, they had established their new political power and also had developed the features of their own new culture, viz. an old Thai animistic substratum with a Mon Buddhist topping: Theravāda Buddhism mixed with slowly diminishing earlier animism; a society of paternal or male dominance mixed with earlier female or maternal prominence that were also slowly diminishing, faster in the aristocracy and slower among the common people. The culture also showed a developed state system that comprised two minorities, Lawa and Mon,[17] had

---

17 Actually we do not know the population figures for Lawa, Mon, and Thai Yuan, but the latter were now the state leaders.

codified laws (see below), and inherited, copied, or developed new techniques and forms, for instance in the fields of pottery and sculpture (see below), and perhaps also in water engineering.

Theravāda Buddhism

The changes in their spiritual life also brought changes in their everyday life. It is probable that soon they began to abandon their old custom of burying the dead and changed to cremation, at first monks and aristocrats, later also the more important commoners. But elements of the old custom of burying were kept: those who lost their life in a "bad death," such as an accident, animal attack, childbirth, or suicide, were interred. The ashes of kings were kept in burial stūpas. For instance, in about 1340 Phayā Phā Yū built a little stūpa on a site that later became Wat Phra Sing in Chiang Mai in order to hold the ashes of his father, Phayā Kham Fū. The remains of the stūpa were opened in 1925 and it still contained three urns with the ashes. The gold, silver, and bronze urns, placed inside each other, have since disappeared. They are presumably lost forever because they very probably were, as the many other objects of precious metal stolen from monasteries and stūpas, melted down to destroy the evidence.

Most common people were buried as before and, if cremated, the ashes were buried in the forest at the foot of a tree. Keeping the ashes in a monastery is a new tradition for Lān Nā, recently imported from central Thailand. Cremation of commoners is said to have become usual only in the nineteenth century.

The early Yuan probably understood Buddhism as another form of magic, and they supported it in order to gain advantage, greatness, victory. Supporting Buddhism was thought to be something that could be traded for personal success in daily life. For instance, Phayā Mang Rāi had five tall wooden Buddha images carved to assure victory before he left on his "visit" to Pegu, and he promised a *wihān* to house them if his expedition was a success. Generally speaking, whatever their earlier preconceptions of Buddhism, living now close to the Mon, their ideas about Buddhism presumably became similar to those of the Mon.

Omens were observed, and chicken bones were studied to foretell future events, such as the outcome of a battle, and to assist in making decisions. That may not have been a newly acquired Brahmanic science but could have been practiced by the Yuan since earlier times; the Chinese also used bone oracles.

Writing

The Yuan began to use two different alphabets and two languages for two different purposes: secular and religious.[18] For secular matters, they continued to use their own traditional Old Thai or Proto Thai script, once presumably adapted from Old Mon, and their Yuan dialect. But for religious purposes, they now used the then modern Mon script called *aksòn tham* อักษรธรรม "*dhamma* letters" (also called *tua müang* ตัวเมือง "local letters") and the Pāli language. Later, they used the *tham* letters also for secular purposes until these characters were universally used throughout

---

18 The Thais at Sukhōthai and generally in central Thailand underwent a similar evolution: they used Thai script / Thai language for secular matters but Khmer script / Pāli language for religious purposes.

Lān Nā and beyond. It speaks for the wide distribution of the *tham* letters that the oldest known specimen is not from Lān Nā but from Sukhōthai.[19]

Their traditional Thai Yuan alphabet,[20] which was similar to the Thai alphabet used in central Thailand, then became restricted chiefly to inscriptions and official or diplomatic documents. It fell into disuse in the decades after 1850 and was replaced by the modern central Thai alphabet. But the rounded *tham* letters, because of their use in religious texts, continued to be widely read and written until about 1950–1960. Though nowadays no longer officially in use, they are still regarded as one of the characteristic features of north Thailand; they are found on nearly all of the many surviving palm-leaf manuscripts and they are taught for scholarly purposes at university level and in some monasteries to uphold the tradition.

To sum up, from this time on the Thai Yuan had two sets of characters or two alphabets: the *fak khām* letters which went back to the Proto Thai letters, and the *tua müang* (*aksòn tham*) which came into existence later under the influence of Lamphūn. Both

---

19 "*Tham*" or "*dhamma*" here means Buddhist teachings, not the brahmanical "dharma" law. These *tham* letters were widely used or at least widely understood. The oldest known document with *tham* letters, an inscription on a gold foil dated 1376, was found in a stūpa in Sukhōthai.

Lān Nā's oldest known palm-leaf manuscript dates from 1471. It is a Jātaka book containing the Vīsati-, Tiṃsa- and Sattati-nipātas, and is written in *tham* letters and Pāli language.

20 There were several slight variants. Perhaps best known, because it was used on many stone inscriptions, is the somewhat slanted and jittery-looking variety called *fak khām* อักษรฝักขาม "tamarind pod letters."

alphabets go back to and were devised from the Mon alphabet, but at different times and also at different places.

When later Lān Nā reached its golden age and became a leading power, many of her cultural features and achievements were exported to neighboring regions with which, since of old, she had been affiliated and shared affinities. Luang Phra Bāng or Lān Chāng (Lāo), Chiang Tung (Thai Khön or Khün, the easternmost Shan States), and Chiang Rung (Thai Lü, Sip-sòng Phan Nā) also took over the *dhamma* or *tham* letters so that present north Thailand, northwest Laos, parts of northeast Burma and parts of southwest China formed an extended area with a similar culture which one might call the "culture of the region of the *dhamma* letters." The similarities are still apparent today.

Chinese art forms

In the fine arts, for instance in stucco decorations and on wall paintings, occasionally Chinese elements appear until perhaps 1500–1550; examples are some fine stucco work in Wiang Kum Kām, wall paintings in Wat Umōng at the foot of Dòi Suthep, and mother-of-pearl work on a wooden Buddhapāda from Chiang Mai's Wat Phra Sing, now in the Chiang Mai museum. Chinese elements of a different type then reappear from about 1850 on.

Law

The Mon had created *dhammasatthas* and *rājasatthas*, collections of more general works on the administration of justice and imaginary stories of cases and decisions. The Yuan, and with them other Thai groups, did not follow the Mon here but took inspiration from them. Their kings wrote up some of the strict traditional rules of their own society, their own customary law, and tried to make it conform to the Dharma and to Theravāda Buddhism. That resulted in a new form of *rājasattha*, i.e. a codex of laws promulgated by the king and binding for all, complete with suggested punishment and also juridical reasoning, sometimes with a short description of a case, therefore a handbook for rulers and judges. It was a codex that was not esoteric but part of public knowledge, also because the details came from real life situations in their own society.

Already Phayā Mang Rāi is said to have governed his country with a code of laws, a *rājasattha* Yuan version, which is usually called *Mang Rāi sāt* มังรายศาสตร์ "Mang Rāi science," that is, Mang Rāi laws. But it is unknown when it was originally composed. Some versions explain that Mang Rāi received it from his father; others say that it was Mang Rāi himself who "set up the laws for worldly affairs without contradicting the dharma" ตั้งอาชญาไว้ตามคดี โลก บ่ห้อผิดคดีธรรม. The law text itself calls the laws, *ātnyā* (S. *ājñā*, P. *āṇā* "order, command") which word in old Lān Nā texts, such as inscriptions, means "royal order."

In the course of time other laws were added to the original items so that the collection grew into a sizable codex of which only the first articles go back to the earliest times even though the whole was still called "Mang Rāi's laws." Since there were a number of smallish but independent kingdoms, it is not surprising that the law codices differed somewhat from one place to the other, though they were basically similar.

Ayuthayā, Lān Nā, and her immediate Thai neighbor Lān Chāng (Luang Phra Bāng) were the only "Indianizing" countries in Southeast Asia to create a code of civil law. Burma, Cambodia, and Champā (central-south Vietnam) did not develop such a code.

Livelihood

There were four main means of living, viz. gathering, hunting, production, and commerce. The first two involved collecting forest products such as honey, lac, and all kinds of animals from insects to deer and fish and snails. Produced goods probably were mainly rice and various vegetables, also cloth, pottery, and iron and bronze objects made from locally mined ore or from bought raw materials. Commerce included all of the above. Apart from the usual little daily village trading, there was medium and long-range trading. Many regions had a revolving market. This meant that some villages had a large market every five days. During the other days the market moved to other villages, for a fixed run, and then returned. Long-range commerce was done in caravans over thousands of kilometers; from Yünnan to south Burma there were several annually traveled routes.

People in lower government service usually were locals who had their own means of living derived from some land or a small business. But higher government officials, who would be moved from time to time to other places, derived their income from local taxes and dues; they also had an income from state rice fields according to their position. A long-range trader had to have an official permit, usually issued by a high authority, if not the king himself. Taxes and dues were collected from goods in transit.

Exemptions could be granted with letters patented under the seal of the ruler. The king probably derived most of his income from commerce, buying and selling at advantageous prices, and on occasion presumably also imposed a royal monopoly.

The Ascent of Lān Nā
1371–1441

1. Overview

The period of expansion and military movements was followed by a period of relative tranquility.

Important changes took place in religion and in the spiritual life of the people in general. Two Ceylon-derived Theravāda schools, both forest-dwellers, entered the country and became highly revered. Their teaching and example slowly began to change the Thai Yuan society but it, by no means, entirely let go of earlier customs.

At the same time industry (celadon, metalwork) seems to have picked up, as well as commerce and mid-distance exports to and imports from neighboring states.

2. Country Affairs

A failed Sukhōthai attack on Phayao and Chiang Mai, c. 1402
This event came about because two situations coincided. One was an irregularity in the succession to the throne of Chiang Mai,

in which someone other than the eldest son was chosen. The other was Sukhothai's freedom from Ayuthayān harassment for a few years, though it was nearing the end of its independence.

Phayā Sän Müang Mā of Chiang Mai (r. probably 1385–1401) let his eldest son, Yī Kum Kām, rule Chiang Rāi but kept his younger son, Sām Fang Kän, with him. Before his death he chose the latter as his successor. The royal officers confirmed him and Sām Fang Kän became king in 1401; he was only thirteen years old. His brother in Chiang Rāi thought he ought to be the king, so he raised an army, attacked Chiang Mai, failed, and took refuge with King Sai Lü in Sukhōthai.[21] He persuaded the Sukhōthai king to go north with an army to help him become king. They first went to seize and plunder Phayao but the inhabitants melted the bronze that covered the roof of a monastery, cast a mighty cannon from it, and defended themselves successfully. Thereupon Sai Lü and Yī Kum Kām went via Chiang Rai and Fāng down to attack Chiang Mai.

They did not beleaguer the town but agreed to a fight with sword and shield between two soldiers from either side; the party of the winner would get Chiang Mai. The winner would be whoever first wounded the other. The Chiang Mai fighter slashed the big toe of the southerner, and Chiang Mai won the duel.

---

21 Mahādharmarāja III, in central Thai sources usually Sai Līdaiya or Sai Lüthai, ruled c. 1398–1419.

The southern army did not immediately break camp but stayed on at the hill Dòi Jet Lin, Sai Lü savoring the water there.[22] Harassed by Chiang Mai soldiers, Sai Lü and Yī Kum Kām finally returned to Chiang Rai, and from there to Sukhōthai. Yī Kum Kām never came back.

Tribute war with the Hò, c. 1403–1405

Tribute to China, viz. to the Hò lord in Yünnan, consisting of rice, had ceased to be paid sometime under King Kü Nā (1367–1388 or 1355–1385), presumably in connection with the end of the Mongol Yüan dynasty in 1368. But under the following Ming dynasty, in about 1403, the Hò lord in Yünnan again exacted the old rice tribute of nine thousand double baskets and, when refused, sent an army to seize Chiang Sän. The Yuan beat them by flinging red-hot sand and pebbles against their body armor of iron, bronze, and leather pieces.

The Hò returned in 1405 when the horoscope for both Chiang Mai and Chiang Sän was bad. However, fate was turned around for the better by various offerings to the horoscope and the spirits, including Mang Rāi. A great thunderstorm wrecked the Hò command post; they retreated, fearing Lān Nā's supernatural powers, and vowed never to return as enemies.

---

22 Dòi Jet Lin ดอย 7 ลิน, "hill with seven water spouts," at the foot of Dòi Suthep opposite the zoo. See below on the foundation of Wiang Jet Lin in 1411.

Governors administrate important city-states

Lān Nā's city-states were administrated by governors who could be commoners or of royal blood. The rank of a governor, even of an important town such as Chiang Sän or Lampāng, was *mün* "ten thousand." Phayao had been annexed in 1338 and presumably was no exception. But when in 1411 Chiang Mai sent its first known governor to Phayao, he held the unique rank of *jao sī mün* เจ้าสี่หมื่น "lord (of) forty thousand." The reason for this extraordinary rank was, as one contemporary inscription puts it, to reward "the foster uncle" อาว์เลี้ยง—for much help in the difficult succession, one is tempted to add. His successors then held the same rank of *sī mün*. Evidently the Phayao post was regarded as prestigious.

Foundation of Wiang Jet Lin, 1411

In the same year 1411 Phayā Sām Fang Kän built Wiang Jet Lin "city with seven water conduits (or water spouts)" at the foot of Dòi Suthep. The Chiang Mai Chronicle says he did so because he took it as an omen that King Sai Lü had had his army camp at the foot of the hill Dòi Jet Lin and that he had gone up to ceremonially wash his hair at the cascade Phā Lāt Luang out of great fear of the Chiang Mai army. Sām Fang Kän had this city built in commemoration of the defeat of the enemy. In later years it served as summer and country residence of the Chiang Mai kings.

Wiang Jet Lin has the unusual shape of a circle with a diameter of about 800 meters. The southeastern section of its mighty earth rampart and broad, water-filled moat at present forms the border between Chiang Mai University and the adjoining arboretum.

When in the 1960s a government pilot farm was built in the central and northern part of the former town, much old brickwork was unearthed including a sizable water basin (now again in use) with a wooden water conduit. That *lin* was a tree trunk cut in half and hollowed out, located about one meter below the soil surface and probably fed by an underground stream.

Nän and Phrä not yet part of Län Nä

Nän, and its dependencies Phrä, Ngäo, and Pua,[23] were still independent but, unlike Chiang Mai, were involved in upheavals and military campaigns. Here is, as an example, a short list of what Nän and Phrä went through within a mere twenty-five years:

- 1376: Nän assists Kamphäng Phet, Sukhöthai's vassal, against an attack from Ayuthayä.
- 1378: Sukhöthai loses its independence and becomes a vassal of Ayuthayä.
- 1393: Sukhöthai and Nän conclude a pact of friendship and mutual assistance; passages of the pact were inscribed in stone and set up in monasteries in both towns. Remains of both stones have been found.
- c. 1399: Phrä seizes Nän and kills its ruler.
- c. 1400: The brother of the ousted Nän ruler returns with an army from Chaliang (Sukhöthai's vassal) and regains power in Nän.

---

23 It is apparent from an inscription of c. 1393 from Nän that the ruler of Nän was also suzerain over Pua, Phrä, and Ngäo.

- 1400: Sukhōthai makes and declares itself independent from Ayuthayā.
- 1400: Sukhōthai seizes Phrä and then releases it to Nān. And then Nān and Phrä's old supporter and master is swallowed by Ayuthayā:
- c. 1410: Sukhōthai again becomes a vassal of Ayuthayā.
- 1438: Sukhōthai becomes a mere province of Ayuthayā.

Obviously, from about 1410 on, both Nān and Phrä were not only independent but also left completely on their own.

3. Everyday Life

Towards a male-oriented society

Lān Nā's ascent in the political domain changed her "international" position and, measured in terms of centuries, was rather short-lived. Her ascent in religious matters changed her society in a way that is still felt today.

As has been shown above, in the old Thai culture the woman had the same standing as the man, and even higher in some matters, if one balances their respective roles or obligations (for example, emphasis on the female line, a new husband joins his wife's family). That slowly changed, on the surface, at least, to a male-dominated culture from about 1300 to 1400 on, in which the woman was relegated to serving the husband—at least that was the ideal in the upper layers of society. Since this was the time when Theravāda Buddhism began to overlay the Thais' former animism, presumably one of the agents that brought about the change were the suttas of the Tipiṭaka, in particular the Jātakas, perhaps especially the Vessantara Jātaka, because they extol Buddhist exemplary behavior. In addition, it seems that the Jātakas, canonically in Pāli language and already quite male-oriented, became even more so in their Thai versions as folktales.

The husband strives for his merit and, ultimately, *nibbāna*, while wife and children have to subordinate themselves, as in the life of Prince Vessantara, the future Buddha Gotama. Although by doing so they also earn a great amount of merit for themselves, the man dominates, gets his will, and in the opinion of the village folks, gets the lion's share of merit.[24]

Hinduism and Brahmanism, two other derivatives of India's patriarchal society, surely played a lesser role here because of their rather small presence in Lān Nā.

This movement towards a male-oriented society was even stronger in central Thailand than in Lān Nā, which kept, until modern times, some old matriarchal features.

---

24 This is an enormous problem for modern Thai society. Buddhist monks and lay scholars will have to find interpretations that are acceptable to modern young people.

But this is not only a problem for the Buddhist society in Thailand. The Middle Ages of Christian Europe had placed their women in a similar submissive or secondary, supporting role, nearly at the same time, and also after a formerly strong position. Here, too, the modern times have found a more equal balance between the roles of man and woman.

The present situation in Thailand seems part of a general human development in which the pendulum is slowly beginning to swing back.

Arrival of the first Lanka-type of Buddhism, 1369–1371: The "Wat Suan Dòk monks"

While the Lamphūn Mon were instrumental in lifting the Yuan to the level of a "high culture," the Yuan began to develop their own new ideas, sought to deepen their knowledge, and then began to exceed their teachers.

Already from about 1330 on, Yuan princes and ordinary people had shown a deep attachment to Buddhism. As one example, they entirely rebuilt Lamphūn's holy stūpa, the Phra Mahā Thāt. As a second example, legend has it that Mang Rāi was drawn to the forest-dwellers and founded, at the foot of Dòi Suthep west of Chiang Mai, the monastery Wat Umōng with its caves for peripatetic meditation, later embellished by his successors. The caves, incidentally, have the radiating arch ("Roman arch"), an architectural feature typical for Lān Nā but hardly known among other Thai groups.

However, neither the Yuan in Lān Nā nor the Siamese in Sukhōthai and Ayuthayā seem to have been fully content with the local, orthodox practice of Buddhism which, in the case of Lān Nā, was derived from the Lamphūn Mon. Phayā Kü Nā tried to find better qualified monks. After inquiries, he invited the *thera* Sumana who lived in Sukhōthai and belonged to a Lanka or Ceylonese sect, to come up and propagate the Buddhism of that school in Lān Nā.

At the time it was held that the monks in Lanka, especially the forest-dwelling (*araññavāsī*) branch of the Mahāvihāra (an otherwise orthodox city-dwelling monastery), had a particular deep knowledge of Buddhism.[25] It was also thought that the Buddhism of Lanka was pure because the acts of the *sangha (sanghakamma),* for instance ordination of new monks, had correctly been conducted since the remote past. According to Lanka tradition, the Buddha had visited here three times, and the Indian monk Mahinda later had brought Buddhism from India to Lanka.

Sumana, who was of Sukhōthai origin, had not in person been to Lanka. He had gone to study with, and had been reordained by, the Mahāthera Udumbara in Martaban, lower Burma, who had studied and had been reordained in Lanka. Sumana thus had received the Lanka traditions second-hand.

When Sumana accepted King Kü Nā's invitation, the king at first invited him to Wat Phra Yün, east of Lamphūn, where he arrived in December 1369. In 1371, Phayā Kü Nā invited him to Chiang Mai and made him the first abbot of the newly founded Wat Suan Dòk west of the town. Sumana and his disciples soon were known as the Suan Dòk school. This was the first recorded attempt at modernizing and deepening Buddhism in Lān Nā.

Thus, at the time of Sumana, there were two sects or schools in Lān Nā: the old city-dwelling sect (*nagaravāsī*) from the time of the Mon, and the new forest-dwelling sect under Sumana with their mother monastery at Wat Suan Dòk, influenced by Lanka, the Sīhaḷa island. But we do not know in what they differed,

---

25 To qualify as a "forest dweller," the monk's monastery or living place must be at least 500 bow lengths from the nearest settlement, approximately 300–500 meters.

except for living in or outside of a settlement. The Suan Dòk school soon found many adherents all over Lān Nā.

In passing it should be mentioned that Sumana's solemn, festive arrival in Lamphūn in 1369 is described in a contemporary stone inscription which is still in Wat Phra Yün, Lamphūn. The inscription is the oldest one in Lān Nā that carries a date (1370) and luckily for us, mentions the orchestra and musical instruments played on that occasion. Among the gongs, drums, trumpets, xylophones, etc. was also the famous bronze kettle drum, *mahōrathük* มโหระทึก. This legendary drum, often associated with hill tribes and prehistoric burials, obviously was then a common Thai musical instrument.

Relations with Pagan

Chiang Mai had not only a spiritual relationship with Sukhōthai but also with Pagan. Though Pagan was now no longer the capital but was part of the kingdom of Ava, even in its decline the Chiang Mai people must have valued it as a religious center.

In 1393, the Mahāthera Mahāsāmi Rājaguru, i.e. the preceptor of the Chiang Mai king (Sän Müang Mā) made his last of altogether three visits to Pagan. He donated in total 375 bāt บาท gold to cover the Shwezigon stūpa with gold leaf, and 400 bāt silver, the interest of which was to be used for a yearly application of lime whitewash of the four smaller stūpas surrounding the principal stūpa. He also left other little sums, the interest of which was to be used for various works, such as polishing Buddha images. We do not know for certain who this high-ranking monk was, perhaps Kumārakassapa, the second abbot of Wat Suan Dòk, the successor to Sumana who had died in 1389.

Obviously there was a well-traveled route between the two places. When King Kü Nā died, says the Chiang Mai Chronicle, he became the guardian spirit of a banyan tree near the road to Pagan which was used by Chiang Mai merchants trading in that town. A certain close relationship is also indicated by the fact that later several monks in Chiang Mai had the epithet *Phūkām* "Pagan" after their name or incorporated in it. Also, two of the early abbots of Wat Suan Dòk had studied in Pagan: Ñāṇaraṅsī, (1443–1450; the sixth abbot) and Buddharakkhita (1456–1468; the eighth abbot).

Beginning of literature

In this period were written or begun the oldest known Lān Nā literary works. They dealt with history and had a strong religious emphasis.

Around 1410 the monk Bodhiraṃsi พระโพธิรังสี translated a history of Lamphūn from Thai into Pāli under the title of Cāmadevīvaṃsa จามเทวีวํศ. He presumably enlarged it with his own, mostly moralistic-religious reflections because the original Yuan texts, as known today, are quite sober and succinct; these manuscripts usually are entitled History of Nāng Jām Thewī ตำนานนางจามเทวี.

He also composed in Pāli the history of the famous Phra Sing Buddha image under the title Sihiṅgabuddharūpanidāna สิหิงคพุทรูบ นิทาน; it is not known on which sources he based his account.

Also another chronicle probably was begun then, and updated from time to time until after 1500: the chronicle of Wat Suan Dòk and its school, Tamnān Mūlasāsanā ตำนานมูลศาสนา, written in the Yuan dialect. Its first author probably was the fourth abbot, Buddhañāṇa พระพุทธญาณ, who was in office c. 1418–1428.

Arrival of the second Lanka-type of Buddhism, 1425–1430: The "Sīhaḷabhikkhus"

The *thera* Sumana's arrival in Chiang Mai in 1371 and his propagation of a Lanka or Sinhalese (Sīhaḷa) type of Buddhism made monks and lay people even more deeply interested in Buddhism. They were no longer content with only going to Martaban in order to study the local "second-hand" Sinhalese Buddhism there as Sumana had done. Now groups of monks and laymen ventured to cross the Indian Ocean and traveled to Lanka for studies directly at the source.[26]

One of the most serious concerns at the time was the purity, even the validity, of the local traditional Buddhism. It was feared that once an ordination ceremony had been flawed, either by incorrect proceedings during the ceremony or by using improper ordination premises (*ubōsot, uposatha, bōt* อุโบสถ, โบสถ์), the newly ordained monk was a false monk, and his participation in future ceremonies would invalidate them as well, with disastrous conse-

---

26 Travel between Chiang Mai and Ceylon was not without danger but neither overly long nor difficult. The shortest way from Chiang Mai to Ceylon is about 2,400 km, which under favorable conditions could have been traveled in about two months. But probably nobody then was in a hurry.

quences for the entire Buddhist order because it would eventually be wiped out.

In 1423 a group of twenty-five monks led by Dhammagambhīra (or Ñāṇagambhira) and Medhaṅkara, plus another group of eight monks from Kamboja under Ñāṇasiddhi, traveled to Lanka. Here they had themselves reordained on the Kalyāṇī River in 1424 by monks from the famous Mahāvihāra monastery according to the most orthodox rites known at the time. They returned to central Thailand in 1425 where they taught and ordained in Ayuthayā, Sukhōthai, and Sachanālai. They reached Chiang Mai in 1430 and settled in Wat Pā Däng at the foot of Dòi Suthep, about 2 km west of Chiang Mai, only about 1 km from Wat Suan Dòk.

From Wat Pā Däng they traveled and propagated their school of forest-dwelling Buddhism throughout Lān Nä and beyond to Chiang Tung and Luang Phra Bäng by founding in select places their own monasteries, typically called "Wat Pā Däng" or "Rattavanamahāvihāra" after the mother monastery in Chiang Mai. The monks called themselves Sīhaḷabhikkhus "Lanka (-type) monks." Their story, from the beginning up to 1527, was recorded by one of their members, the *thera* Ratanapañña, in the famous chronicle Jinakālamālī.

In all of Lān Nä, the monks of this new, later or second Sinhalese school were called Wat Pā Däng monks and the monks of the old or first Sinhalese school, going back to Sumana, were called Wat Suan Dòk monks to distinguish one group from the other.

Thus, there were now three sects or schools, all of the Theravāda branch of Buddhism. In chronological order they were, (1) the old town-dwelling sect (Nagaravāsī), which went back to Mon times, and then the two newer forest-dwelling schools, (2) the Suan Dòk monks (Pupphavāsī), and (3) the Wat Pā Däng monks (Sīhaḷabhikkhus). They were not equal in numbers as can be seen from the following example. In 1515 (i.e. about eighty years later) the three sects conducted ordinations in Chiang Sän under the sponsorship of Phayā Käo: 235 Wat Pā Däng monks, 370 town-dwelling monks, and 1,011 Wat Suan Dòk monks. This means that the newer Suan Dòk sect had by far overtaken the older city-dwelling sect, and that the Wat Pā Däng monks were a minority.

The most learned group certainly were the Wat Pā Däng monks (the Sīhaḷabhikkhus) who soon were highly esteemed by kings and the better instructed. We know some of the points in which they differed from the other two schools. There was the problem of the validity of ordination, concerning which the Sīhaḷabhikkhus held that theirs was the only one surely valid, while the ordination of the other two sects was doubtful if not downright invalid. They themselves, until much later, conducted their own ordinations only on boats in the river, to avoid possible spiritual contamination because of incorrectly delimited premises.

On a more practical note, they held that their pronunciation in reciting religious texts was correct, and that it was not permissible to carry a stick and wear the robe in the open mode (i.e. one shoulder uncovered) when walking for alms. The Sīhaḷabhikkhus therefore kept apart from the other monks.

Especially at the beginning they were in heated argument and once even got into a fight with their co-brethren of the Wat Suan Dòk sect. That was a great scandal since Lān Nā's monks traditionally were inoffensive and acted with self-restraint. The quarrels were so upsetting in Chiang Mai and Chiang Tung that rulers of both towns had to interfere in person, with the monarchs of both places consulting each other and agreeing on a common "strategy." The Sīhaḷabhikkhus were even temporarily banned from the city of Chiang Mai. But it seems that nobody called this split a schism, or *sanghabheda*, the most heinous crime to be committed against the Buddhist order.

Later, tempers settled, and perhaps by about 1550–1600 the controversial points seemed less important and quietly "disappeared," perhaps also because the Wat Pā Däng sect slowly diminished in numbers. In the end the differences between all three sects became less and less noticeable and the *sangha* again formed one body.

Whatever great influence Lanka had on Lān Nā's monks, the monks did not blindly follow Lanka's Buddhism but kept to certain features of their own traditions. For instance, in Lān Nā, the most important part of the cult was and remained the Buddha image. In Ceylon, the image would rank only perhaps fourth after a Buddha relic, a Bodhi tree, and a Buddha footprint.

A wave of construction of Buddhist monasteries began. In 1411, for example, the already mentioned governor of Phayao built a large monastery, Wat Phra Suwanna Mahā Wihān, and caused the foundation of forty-two filial monasteries, for all of which he donated the principal Buddha image. Why exactly forty-two, is not apparent—it was perhaps his age. The ruins of some of these filial monasteries have been located; one is at present still an active monastery.

Underlying old animism and magic

Although the educated class were in search of an "improved" or even "pure" Buddhism, a strong belief in spirits and magic continued parallel to Buddhism. Phayā Sām Fang Kän, for instance, built an important monastery, but he also reverently worshiped all sorts of things and spirits; the chronicle Jinakālamālī complains that he honored demon-followers and sacrificed cattle and buffaloes to worship (the spirits of?) groves, trees, heaped mounds, hills, and forests.

When Phayā Kü Nā had died, it was believed that his soul(s) could not find rest. It became a tree spirit and whispered to two traders, who were resting under the tree, that a very tall *jedī* should be erected in the town and the merit transferred to him. This was the beginning, in c. 1391, of the future Jedī Luang in Chiang Mai. How much even such a fervent Buddhist as the mighty Phayā Tilōk, and his equally fervent Ayuthayā opponent Trailōkanāt, relied on such supernatural powers will be related in the next chapter.

These examples show a double form or a double standard of spiritual life, viz. inclination towards pure Buddhism (which denies or ignores the role of magic and ghosts) and inclination towards magic or supernatural powers, animistic beliefs and practices to achieve a worldly aim in a tit-for-tat barter of the type, "I offer you this and you will get me that." This certainly was historical and not an addition to the chronicles by later copyists. Ratanapañña who reported about Phayā Sām Fang Kän in his chronicle Jinakālamālī, lived less than one hundred years after the king and thus probably knew the stories well.

Celadon manufacture

It is probable that Mons and Thais produced pottery for hundreds if not thousands of years. But it is only in this time that we have the first two dated celadon kilns (1420 and 1455) from the so-called Inthakhin kiln complex near Mä Täng, about 30 km north of Chiang Mai. Since a couple of kilns are beneath the ones that could be dated, it is certain that a Thai Yuan potters' village existed here since about 1350, at the latest. The kilns were single-chambered, above-ground, and cross-draft kilns. They produced jars, plates, and bowls with a green and brown glaze. Later kiln complexes have been found all over Lān Nā; fourteen are known at present. Obviously the Yuan produced enough pots and other vessels for their own local demand, and had enough left over for sale and trade.

The oldest dated Buddha images, 1427

Nān and Phrä then passed through difficult political and military times before they came under Chiang Mai's administration as part of Lān Nā. Yet cultural and religious life flourished. In 1427, probably to make merit on the occasion of his accession to the Nān throne, Somdet Jao Phayā Lāra Phä Sum สมเด็จเจ้าพญาลาร ผาสุม had the means to cast five exquisite bronze Buddha statues in the Sukhōthai post-classical style; they are slightly taller than life size. One has been lost but the others can still be seen in Wat Phayā Phū and Wat Chāng Kham. Three of them still have their pedestals that carry dated inscriptions. They show the Buddha walking and standing and are today the oldest known dated images from Lān Nā, though administratively speaking Nān was not yet part of Lān Nā.

The Golden Age of Lān Nā
1441–1526

1. Overview

The period of Lān Nā's build-up, which lasted for about 170 years from about 1280 to 1450, was followed by Lān Nā's golden age, which lasted for about seventy-five years, from about 1450 to about 1525. That corresponds to the beginning of the reign of Phayā Tilōka Rāt in 1441 and the end of the reign of Phayā Käo in 1526, which two years therefore can be taken as markers. During this period Lān Nā reached its greatest extent, also perhaps its best economic position, becoming known for her "quality of life" as we would say today, and achieving a general cultural, religious apogée.

Because Lān Nā was a conglomerate of city-states, the power of the overlord who ruled from Chiang Mai did not end at a fixed border but faded gradually with increased distance from Chiang Mai. Such a situation could make the position of an outlying state ambiguous. Chiang Tung, for example, was not directly under Chiang Mai and thus was not part of the inner core of the Lān Nā city-states, the kingdom of Lān Nā, yet it had strong ties with Chiang Mai. Similarly, Luang Phra Bāng was close to Chiang Mai without being "under" Chiang Mai. Further in the north and northwest, the influence of the prosperity and civilization of Chiang Mai reached to Chiang Rung, Möng Nāi (Moné), and Möng Mīt. The king of Chiang Mai could hardly expect his orders to be obeyed in these places. But what went on in Chiang Mai certainly was noted there.

Thus, Lān Nā was not a country with sharply defined borders but was rather a group of city-states that were directly under Chiang Mai and its administration. On the outskirts there was a ring of bigger and smaller city-states that maintained more or less close relations with Chiang Mai so that the latter's power and culture reached these *müang* as well. One could perhaps say that the ruler of the city-state Chiang Mai ruled over the surrounding city-states by his own power; all of these states formed Lān Nā proper. But he also had prestige and therefore influence on a second and more outlying, surrounding ring of city-states.

Such a configuration, i.e. a core with peripheral states, where the actual political power soon diminishes beyond the core while the cultural power and influence extend much farther into the periphery, was probably not unique. A similar configuration has been suggested for Dvāravatī, a city-state conglomerate in central Thailand between approximately 600 and 1100.

2. Country Affairs

Tilōk and Trailōkanāt

Lān Nā's golden age began soon after the accession of her most powerful king, Phayā Tilōka Rāt, or Tilōk for short (r. 1441–1487), who in 1441 coerced his father, Sām Fang Kän, to abdicate and to hand the country over to him. The sources do not give a reason for this event even though the Chiang Mai Chronicle reports it in detail.

About the first half of Lān Nā's golden age falls in the reign of Tilōk. He must have been a man of contradictory character traits, and historians have difficulty describing and evaluating many of his acts. On the one hand, he led Lān Nā on the way to her peak in the arts and letters and state power, and he also was deeply religious both in the Buddhist and magic-Brahmanical way; on the other hand, he involved his country continuously in "useless" and "inconclusive" raids and wars and seemed overly brutal. He must have been both clever and naive.

It so happened that in his lifetime, Ayuthayā also had a powerful and dynamic monarch, King Phra Bòròma Trailōkanāt (r. 1448–1488).[27] He and Tilōk were life-long antagonists. Tilōk was eager to seize Sukhōthai provinces, if not Sukhōthai itself, from Trailōkanāt; and the latter was equally eager to add one or two of Lān Nā's southern provinces to his own possessions. Curiously, the latter's Sanskrit regnal title *Trailokanātha* "Protector of the Three Worlds" was similar to the Pāli title of his opponent, *Tilokarāja* "King of the Three Worlds."

King Trailōkanāt of Ayuthayā was a great creator of laws. Central Thailand and later Siam owe him, among other things, the definite versions of the laws governing the *sakdi nā* grade (1454),[28] and also the *Kot monthian bān* "Palace Law," promulgated in 1450.

---

27 During 1448–1463 his court was in Ayuthayā, 1463–1488 in Phitsanulōk.

28 A system that grades persons according to their social standing by assigning them imaginary or honorary ownership of rice fields. Even the poorest person still had the grade of "five" (honorary fields). It was useful, and chiefly used, for administrative purposes.

The latter begins with an enumeration of states that sent tribute to Ayuthayā. Surprisingly, among them are Sän Wī (Hsen Wi, in the Shan States), Chiang Tung, Chiang Mai, and Taungu. That does not mean that Chiang Mai and the other states were under Ayuthayā at the time. Obviously these states were not included in the original version of the law but added later, perhaps around 1600 when Siam briefly controlled west Lān Nā, or towards the end of the eighteenth or in the nineteenth century when what is now north Thailand was joined to central Thailand, or Siam.

Ayuthayā tries an invasion, 1442–1443

Tilōk's accession met with internal opposition. In 1442–1443, an official invited Bòròmarāja II of Ayuthayā (father of the future king Trailōkanāt) per letter to attack Chiang Mai. The Ayuthayā forces came up with the vassal rulers of Sukhōthai and Kamphäng Phet. The Chiang Mai troops beat them back, and when Bòròma-rāja fell ill, the Ayuthayā forces withdrew. A Sukhōthai prince, Yuthisathian,[29] arranged for Bòròmarāja to escape safely, and then fought valiantly and took charge of the rearguard. This prince, then perhaps not much more than sixteen years old, would later emigrate to Lān Nā and play an important part in the relations between central Thailand and Lān Nā.

---

29 ยุทธิเสถียร. Northern writings such as the Chiang Mai Chronicle usually call him Yuthisathiang.

The annexation of Phrä, 1443/44, and Nān, 1448/49

The reason for Tilōk's campaign against Phrä is unknown. Perhaps it was because on the way to Nān and was always more or less connected with Nān.

The reasons given in our sources for the war against Nān differ widely. According to the Nān Chronicle, the Nān ruler had sent a load of salt from the famous Bò Klüa salt wells to Tilōk who thereupon greedily wished to annex Nān. But according to the Chiang Mai Chronicle, the ruler of Nān had asked for an army from Tilōk to assist against an outside enemy, and then had treacherously murdered many of the Chiang Mai men during a banquet.

In November 1443 Tilōk and his mother set out to conquer and annex Nān. Phrä, which lay on their way, could not immediately be seized, so they went on to Nān.

From Nān Tilōk sent his mother with a force back to Phrä. Under her command a Käo[30] in Yuan government service proved very useful. His work had to do with rice fields *nā* and therefore he had the title Phan Lām Nā พันล่ามนา. But since his personal name was Pān Songkhrām ป้านสงคราม "the war Pān," he evidently was no stranger to warfare. He took over as gunner and shot a terrifying device called "lord grandfather *pün* ปืนปู่เจ้า (either a big crossbow or a fire weapon)[31] repeatedly so well into a tree that the Phrä governor was intimidated and surrendered. The date is

---

30 The Käo แก้ว are understood in Lān Nā to be North Vietnamese, but their exact ethnicity remains unclear.

31 Pün is the modern word for a fire weapon; before their advent in the fifteenth century it meant an arrow.

not known; it was probably December 1443 or early 1444. The queen mother let him continue to govern Phrä as before.

Nän was not so easily conquered. Tilōk finally overcame the defenses only about five years later, in 1448 or 1449. Here a cannon (*amòk sīnāt* อะม๊อกสีนาด) is said to have been used. The defeated Nän ruler fled to Sachanālai. Tilōk replaced him with the ruler's son who died in 1459. From then on Nän was administrated by a governor appointed from Chiang Mai.

During this period of transition, Luang Phra Bāng attacked Nän after Tilōk had returned to Chiang Mai in 1449, but in the end their troops were defeated by two Lān Nä contingents.

Prince Yuthisathian of Phitsanulōk emigrates to Lan Nä, 1452

In the course of time several foreign rulers placed themselves under the umbrella of Lān Nä's rulers, and some princes with large groups of followers even emigrated to Lān Nä; for instance in 1517 the lords of Müang Nāi (Moné, in the Shan States) and of Chiang Thòng (not identified). Not all were successful: the governor of Nakhòn Thai and his group, in 1462, on their way from central Thailand to Nän, were pursued by the Ayuthayā minister of war in person (*klāhōm* กลาโหม), were caught and forcibly brought back. Obviously the rulers of Lān Nä and their country were much esteemed abroad.

Perhaps the most important of these foreign immigrant princes was Prince Yuthisathian of Phitsanulōk, already mentioned. To better understand the events that led to the departure from his homeland, it is necessary to retrace a little the history of Sukhō-thai, Phitsanulōk, and Ayuthayā.

Within sixty years, between 1378 and 1438, the city-state and kingdom of Sukhōthai was overthrown and torn down in stages. In 1378 the king of Sukhōthai lost three of his four bastion cities (Nakhòn Sawan, Phitsanulōk, Kamphäng Phet; left only was Sachanālai) in battle to Ayuthayā, was taken prisoner, and was forced to become a vassal of Ayuthayā. Sukhōthai regained independence in 1400 for a short time but was again reduced to vassalage around 1410. In 1438, with the death of the last ruler, it became a mere province of Ayuthayā and ceased to exist as a kingdom. In the 1420s, the last king of Sukhōthai had transferred his court to Phitsanulōk which thus was the final capital of the Sukhō-thai kingdom.

In 1438 King Bòròmarācha II of Ayuthayā (whom northern sources call Sām Phayā) sent his young son, Rāmesuan, as viceroy to Phitsanulōk; the prince was perhaps only about seven years old. When the new viceroy went to venerate the huge Buddha image named Phra Phuttha Chinarāt (Jinarāja) in Phitsanulōk, it is reported in a chronicle, the image shed tears. It supposedly grieved that the old kingdom of Sukhōthai was now being incorporated into the kingdom of Ayuthayā.

One of Ramesuan's local vassals, scion of the old ruling family of Sukhōthai, was Prince Yuthisathian, who presumably was not much older, perhaps in his early teens. They became friends. The young viceroy Rāmesuan promised Yuthisathian that when he should succeed to the throne of Ayuthayā, he would make Yuthisathian his successor as viceroy, ruling half of the kingdom.

Yuthisathian was a loyal vassal and later distinguished himself in Ayuthayā's failed Chiang Mai invasion of 1442–1443, as has been told above.

However, when Rāmesuan did become king in 1448, with the regnal name Phra Bòròma Trailōkanāt, he made Yuthisathian merely governor of Phitsanulōk. Yuthisathian felt slighted and, wishing to transfer his allegiance to Chiang Mai, he asked Tilōk how he would address him. The reply came that Tilōk would call him "son," and the matter was concluded.

In 1452 Tilōk led an army south, Yuthisathian opened the gates of Phitsanulōk to him, and the occupying Ayuthayā forces, if there were any, probably were taken by surprise.

Both then undertook a roving campaign seizing other Sukhōthai cities in the vicinity, and even tried, in vain, to capture Sukhōthai. But they had to halt because news came that Lān Chāng (Luang Phra Bāng) was going to attack Chiang Mai. Presumably also Ayuthayā was recovering from the surprise. Tilōk and Yuthisathian seemingly could not hold their conquests, not even Phitsanulōk, and so both returned north, taking ten thousand of Yuthisathian's followers with them, along with a considerable number of elephants, horses, slaves, and much personal property. On their way they were attacked by vassals loyal to Ayuthayā, notably by the governor of Sachanālai who succeeded in seizing back one thousand of Yuthisathian's followers, thus about 10 percent. They were in grave danger, and it was only due to Tilōk's mounted crossbowmen or archers who counterattacked and shot poisoned arrows, that they did not perish there.

Safely back in Lān Nā, Tilōk made Yuthisathian governor of the Phan Nā ("district") Phū Khā in the Pua region north of Nān, and then governor of Phayao.

By 1452 the state of affairs was therefore that neither Ayuthayā nor Chiang Mai had gained territory from the other, but that Chiang Mai had otherwise gained enormously with the immigration of Prince Yuthisathian and his followers.

Phitsanulōk was not annexed to Lān Nā. It remained under Ayuthayā, and Trailōkanāt appointed a new governor to replace Yuthisathian.

Ayuthayā / Sukhōthai raids and counter-raids, 1456–1463

During the next few years both antagonists were otherwise busy, Tilōk sending raiding parties to the east towards the Luang Phra Bāng region on the Mä Khōng (1454) and north into Chiang Rung territory (1455, 1456). But the following years between 1456 and c. 1463 must have been filled with dramatic events, both in southern Lān Nā and in the northern part of the Sukhō-thai province, because the chronicles as we have them obviously muddle and slightly misdate exciting events.

In 1456 Trailōkanāt probably tried to raid south Lān Nā. A chronicle says that he went to seize Müang Li Sop Thin เมือง ลิสบทิน "Müang Li at the mouth of the Thin River" and that he established his personal camp at Tambon Khōn ตำบลโคน. This is geographically doubtful but sounds much like present Lī and Thōn, south of Lamphūn and north of Tāk; Khōn has been identi-fied as a place on the Mä Ping, about halfway between Kamphäng

Phet and Nakhòn Sawan. But nothing is said about the outcome of the expedition, so perhaps he was not successful.

Trailōkanāt, strengthened with troops from Sukhōthai and Kamphäng Phet, tried again in 1457, the aim being to seize Chiang Mai. Coming up via Lampāng, he was beaten back at Lampāng in a night battle, where Yuthisathian greatly distinguished himself for his new overlord Tilōk and against his former people, fighting three elephant duels against Crown Prince Intharāchā of Ayuthayā (who would have been about ten years old!) and the lords of Sukhōthai and Kamphäng Phet. The crossbowmen shot salvos, and Prince Intharāchā was hit in the face, which left him with a big scar. The southern army then withdrew. A valiant general on this occasion was Mün Dong Nakhòn of Lampāng. Phayā Tilōk and the crown prince, Bun Rüang, were present during the battle.

The year 1458 was used, by order of Tilōk, to grow rice under Mün Nòi Dam Phrā. Obviously the barns were seriously depleted and had also to be replenished in view of future military campaigns.

In January 1460 Tilōk besieged Trailōkanāt and his vassal lord of Kamphäng Phet for a long time in Phitsanulōk. The reason for this campaign is unknown. The Lān Nā army did not intend to or could not take the town. Finally Trailokanāt and the lord of Kamphäng Phet escaped from the city by night. But Tilōk did not seriously pursue Trailōkanāt and restrained Mün Dong with the words, "He is a king, I am a king. We defeated them, and they are ashamed. Don't go after them." He also does not seem to have given administrative orders for the annexation of Phitsanu-lōk. Instead, he returned to Chiang Mai. Here he rewarded Yuthisathian with the additional governorships of the city-states Ngāo "(of the) Kāo people" เมืองงาวกาว, as a chronicle says, and Phrä.

The annexation of Sachanālai, c. 1460

In about 1460 Tilōk got hold of Sachanālai[32] more by accident than by intent. His raids in the east and north had somewhat expanded his possessions, but this was by far his most important acquisition. The dates of this episode are slightly uncertain because of differences in the sources.

As the Chiang Mai Chronicle tells it, in 1459 Tilōk went north to attack Thai Lü domains. Trailōkanāt heard that the Chiang Mai army was absent, so he led his army against Phrä. But here he was met by an army under Mün Dong of Lampāng, and then by another army under Tilōk who in the meantime had returned from the Lü country. Trailōkanāt therefore withdrew very fast to Ayuthayā, pursued by the northerners who could not catch him. Arriving at Sachanālai, they intended to capture the city. The governor of Sachanālai was very afraid of the Lān Nā army and submitted as vassal to Tilōk. Tilōk then attacked Phitsanulōk in vain, returned to Sachanālai, reinstated the former governor, now his vassal, and returned to Chiang Mai. Mün Dong Nakhòn and another official, Lām Mün Wiak, were to take care of administra-

---

32 The old, walled town at the cascades on the Yòm River, famous for its celadon pottery, has been known under many names. At present it is called Old Sī Sachanālai; former names include Sachanālai, Chaliang, Chiang Chün, Sangkhalōk (hence the name of the pottery) and Sawankhalōk. I use "Sachanālai" throughout and sometimes add in brackets the name used by a source in a particular episode.

tive country matters รั้วเมือง. Sachanālai had easily become a part of Lān Nā.

Two years later, in 1461, the governor of Sachanālai had a change of heart and intended to kill Mün Dong during a cock fight in Sachanālai. But he was caught and exiled to Müang Hāng where he later died. Mün Dong of Lampāng now also became the governor of Sachanālai.

No doubt part of the former Sukhōthai towns were then in revolt against Ayuthayā. The unsuccessful emigration in 1462 of the people of Nakhòn Thai to Nān has already been mentioned. It was a passive revolt against Ayuthayā.

Also Sukhōthai must have sided with Chiang Mai and joined in a revolt against Ayuthayā because in the same year, 1462, the Ayuthayā minister of war (*klāhōm* กลาโหม) in person was sent to attack and reduce it again to submission.

The north of the Ayuthayā kingdom thus under pressure, Trailōkanāt in 1463 bravely transferred his court into the danger area, viz. to Phitsanulōk, and made it his new capital. He therefore switched places with his son, Intharāchā, and sent him to govern Ayuthayā, where the son assumed the regnal title Bòròmarāchā (the future Phra Bòròmarāchā III).

The failed annexation of Sukhōthai, 1463

The Luang Prasöt Chronicle of Ayuthayā, but not the Chiang Mai Chronicle, says that in 1463 Tilōk went with an army to seize Sukhōthai. Trailōkanāt and his son, Intharāchā (Bòròmarāchā), successfully defended the town. Mün Nakhòn, the governor of Lampāng, had an elephant duel with Intharāchā. It was a great battle with at one time four northern elephants encircling the one single southern royal elephant. Prince Intharāchā of Ayuthayā was (again!) wounded in the face by an arrow or bullet ต้องปืน ณ พระพักตร์, but in the end the northern army withdrew.

Trailōkanāt's first sorcery stratagem, 1465–1466

Trailōkanāt of Ayuthayā, now ruling from Phitsanulōk, became a temporary monk from June 1465 to March 1466 in the newly built Wat Julāmanī south of Phitsanulōk. His son Intharāchā was regent in the meantime. Before his ordination he sent envoys asking Tilōk for friendship สัญชัยไมตรี. This was refused, but another request for the Eight Requisites[33] and a chapter of monks for the ordination was granted, Tilōk sending him twelve forest-dwelling monks. The kings of Luang Phra Bāng (Lān Chāng) and Pegu (Hongsāwadī) also sent him the Eight Requisites. A monk from Lanka was present at his ordination.

While a monk, Trailōkanāt actively continued scheming. For one, he sent a message to Tilōk asking for the province of Sachanālai (Chaliang) as alms-food. Tilōk had a mixed committee of monks and state elders consider the request, who decided that it was quite improper, coming from a king who was now a monk.

Trailōkanāt next hired a Burmese monk or white-clad ascetic, *chī mān* ชีม่าน, from Pagan who was strong in magic รู้สัพพสาสตรสิลป์ สิปปคุณ มากนัก, to destroy Tilōk and Chiang Mai. That person persuaded Tilōk, if he wanted to be a *cakkavatti* "universal monarch" like (the Indian king) Aśoka and ruler over all of Jambudīpa, he

---

33 Robes, alms bowl, etc.

must build a new palace in the northeast of the town where the huge banyan tree was standing, the *sī müang* ศรีเมือง "auspicious glory of the country." For that, the city wall had to be dismantled there, the moat filled in, and all the trees chopped down. Tilōk, who presumably wanted to equal Aśoka somehow,[34] agreed. The palace was finished in 1466, the palace toilet built at the spot where the *sī müang* tree had been standing, and the entire new settlement was named Sī Phūm ศรีภูมิ by the Pagan monk. Also, a new gate was built there, the Sī Phūm Gate. Then the monk and the state officials consecrated Tilōk with power to subdue the continent similar to Aśoka, and he ceremonially entered his new palace.[35]

The wrongful execution of Tilōk's son, c. 1466–1470

The Chiang Mai Chronicle observes that from then on all kinds of calamities befell the country and its inhabitants. The historical epos *Lilit Yuan Phāi* says Tilōk suspected personal enemies everywhere and acted as if he were mad, *bā* บ้า.[36]

---

34 An inscription from Phayao dated 1478 calls him Phra Rācha Aśoka Rāt, i.e. Aśokarāja พระราชอโศกราช "King Aśoka."

35 The northeastern corner of the old walled town of Chiang Mai is still called Jäng ("city corner") Sī Phūm. The Sī Phūm gate must have been closed later because it no longer exists.

36 The *Lilit Yuan Phāi* "Poem on the Defeat of the Yuan" says that he acted as if he were mad after he had gotten Sachanālai (Chiang Chün). He suspected treason everywhere and feared that someone would snatch the power from him. For that reason he had his son killed and later even the capable and faithful governor and general, Mün Dong Nakhòn.

It probably was in the years 1466–1470, after the new palace had been built, that a royal princess named Jao Mä Thāo Hò Muk[37] accused Tilōk's son Bun Rüang of some misdeed. Bun Rüang was governor of Chiang Rāi and had fought at Lampāng (1457) and at Phitsanulōk (1460). Thus accused, Tilōk exiled him to Müang Nòi, near present Pāi. Later she pushed Tilōk to kill him. Only afterwards was it found that he was innocent.

Our sources are vague as to what his crime was, and when and where Bun Rüang died. Ayuthayā sources say that Tilōk feared his son would usurp the power from him, which is why he had him killed, or that Bun Rüang actually succeeded in snatching the power from Tilōk. The Chiang Mai Chronicle has no details about his crime nor execution, but has an entry saying that in 1470 a *Mün* Bun Rüang, governor of Chiang Rāi, died in "the Ngio country,"[38] which may or may not be an error for *Thāo* Bun Rüang.

It also happened now that an innocent brave warrior was executed on the basis of a found letter that advocated a revolt against Tilōk but which in reality had been faked with his stolen personal seal. Tilōk later learned the truth and ordered that from then on no "found" letters should be considered, which became permanent law.

---

37 Compared with the full name or title of his son, Jao Phò Thāo Bun Rüang, she must have been a royal princess of the highest rank, probably either the daughter of Tilōk or the daughter of his father, King Sām Fang Kän.

Some modern scholars understand that she was the wife of Tilōk; others say that she was his daughter but took her as his wife and committed the grave sin of incest.

38 The Ngio country would be any of the Shan states west and north of Mä Hòng Sòn, excluding Chiang Tung.

Trailōkanāt's second sorcery stratagem, c. 1466–1468

Trailōkanāt now sent a Yunnanese Muslim sorcerer, *phā sī*,[39] who interred pots with magic contents in the six city gates and the center of the city. Then Trailōkanāt sent envoys with presents and a missive, but in reality to find out how far the sorcerers had come with their work of destruction.

Tilōk and his people, who were suspicious, employed counter-magic. The Yunnanese was caught and revealed all: the machinations of the Burmese sorcerer, his own doings, and the true role of the envoys. The Burmese magician-monk and the Yunnanese Muslim sorcerer were incarcerated. The envoys were invited to a reception with banquet, during which one of the envoys stole a golden cup. This was reported to Tilōk. The two sorcerers were then thrown into some Mä Ping rapids, and the envoys were killed on their return to the south.

Lān Nā loses Sachanālai, 1475

In 1474 Mün Dong Nakhòn died, the capable governor of Lampāng, who was also in charge of Sachanālai; possibly he was killed on Tilōk's order.[40] This entailed a rotation of governors of several cities. Directly following the installation of a new governor in Sachanālai, Trailōkanāt brought an army up and recaptured in

---

39 ผาสี perhaps lit. "white turban."

40 The Chiang Mai Chronicle only says that he died. But the epos Lilit Yuan Phāi says that Tilōk had him killed because he feared that the Mün would unseat him. His wife, who was in Sachanālai (Chiang Chün) at the time, and many others there were so embittered that they went over to the Ayuthayā king.

a battle the town from the Thai Yuan, probably in early 1475.[41] The Ayuthayā crown prince Intharāchā was wounded in the face during that battle.

Since Intharāchā can hardly have been wounded three times in the same way (in 1457 at Lampāng, six years later in 1463 at Sukhōthai, and now again eight years later in 1475 at Sachanālai), the modern reader is left to wonder which details of these campaigns to believe, and how many campaigns there really were, and when.

In the same year or the next, 1476, Tilōk and Trailōkanāt concluded peace. Sachanālai had been with Lān Na for thirteen to fifteen years, from around 1460 and 1462, to 1475.

Kāo try to settle at Nān, 1480

There may have been a continuing small-scale influx of outsiders into Lān Nā. In 1480 an unexplained and rather large incursion happened when a strong group of Kāo battled their way past "Müang Chawā," i.e. Luang Phra Bāng, arrived at the Nān frontier, and forcefully tried to settle in Nān territory.

They came with their families, elephants, and horses but were not accepted by the Nān governor, Thāo Khā Kān, who opposed them in a brutal military action, cutting heads off and sending them to Tilōk with prisoners taken. Enraged, they refused to leave. The Yuan now intended to build a giant crossbow (*nā mai* หน้าไม้) with a span of about 5.5 meters firing missiles larger than a fist,

---

41 This battle is the main topic of the historical epos *Lilit Yuan Phāi* "Defeat of the Yuan."

but before it was finished a list got rid of the newcomers. Two Hò, who claimed "we and the Käo understand each other," asked for an honorarium of 1000 weight silver (c. 1.1 kg) from Tilōk for talking them into leaving peacefully. Tilōk took up the offer and the Hò succeeded with a ruse: they spread the lie among the Käo that mighty Yuan armies were on their way. The Käo withdrew.

It is here that we can take a glimpse at the statesman Tilōk. He was not satisfied with the action of the Nān governor, declaring that (1) he should have let the Käo escape instead of killing and capturing them and their families, and (2) the Käo prisoners should not be allowed to settle in Nān. Then he transferred the governor to Chiang Rāi.

Perhaps this was the same incursion by Vietnamese which elsewhere is dated 1471 and given a curious reason: the country Pa-pe (Lān Nā?) was invaded by the king of Tonking, Ki-Hao, who was in hot pursuit of a son of the king of Lān Chāng (Luang Phra Bāng). He also tried to obtain the help of the prince of Chöli (Chiang Tung), but the king of Pa-pe repulsed the invaders.

The China / Yünnan tribute, c. 1480

The Käo incursion led to a diplomatic exchange with China, or rather with Yünnan, and shows that until this time Lān Nā was in a way dependent on Yünnan's goodwill.

Tilōk, who did not want the Käo prisoners in his country, made a present of them to the Hò Chinese governor of Yünnan, whom the Chiang Mai Chronicle calls Jao Lum Fā เจ้าลุ่มฟ้า "lord under the sky," that is, "lord of the earth," and places him in "Müang Videha," i.e. Yünnan, or perhaps more precisely, at Dali or Kunming. This dignitary was impressed with Tilōk's victory over the Käo and raised the status of Tilōk. For the diplomatic protocol, he increased his rank from a lord of a hundred thousand men to a lord of a million men เจ้าพลล้าน. He also had a document drawn up and kept in the Gold Hall Archives that declared Tilōk to be the overlord in the west while he, Jao Lum Fā, was the overlord in the east. Then he sent Tilōk an investiture patent as vassal ruler, a *lāi jum lāi jia* ลายจุมลายเจีย "written document with seal," which asked that, if enemies came to threaten him as the Jao Lum Fā, the Lān Nā king would summon his various local lords with their troops and suppress them.[42]

Some time later Jao Lum Fā called for tribute, *sen kung khòng kan* เส้นกุ้งของกัน. One source says that he demanded 5,000 hāp หาบ "twin loads" of iron (150 t)[43] and 100,000 weight in gold (c. 110 kg), which, even if exaggerated, shows Lān Nā as a producer of (pig) iron and gold. Tilōk refused, arguing that if he had to send that much, he would not have enough left to defeat the enemies of the Jao Lum Fā, as laid down in his investiture patent. An exchange of polite diplomatic messages followed, the Jao Lum Fā dispensed Tilōk from tribute, and Tilōk in the end did send, not "tribute," but *bannākān* บรรณาการ "gifts," consisting of nine

42 *Lāi jum* is really the seal but also any document with official seal attached; *lāi jia* is a paper document (*jia* "paper"). Actually, China did not so much "invest" as affirm or recognize a ruler.

43 *Hāp* means goods carried by one person at the two ends of a shoulder pole. In the nineteenth century the standard Chinese *hāp* was 30 kg, but the standard Thai *hāp* was double, 60 kg or 1 picul, which here would amount to 300 t.

elephant tusks, nine pieces of Burmese cloth, nine pieces of Thai cloth, and nine rhinoceros horns.[44]

This was the end of Län Nä's tribute to China.

The Lampäng conspiracy, 1486

Tilōk's fear of a conspiracy against him was not unfounded. In 1486 five high officials plotted for unknown reasons to depose Tilōk and to replace him with one Mün Wiang Din, otherwise unknown. The conspiracy was discovered and three of the main leaders were executed, among them the governors of Phräo and Chiang Rāi.

Abdication and death of Tilōk, 1487

Tilōk, now about seventy-eight years old and probably ill, abdicated in early May 1487, choosing as successor his grandson, Yòt Chiang Rāi, since he had ordered his son Bun Rüang killed about twenty years before. The state officials confirmed his choice. Tilōk died not long thereafter, towards the end of the same month. His

---

44 A letter of the fifteenth century from the ruler of Län Nä to the Chinese emperor, asking for recognition after the death of his father, and accompanying tribute, mentions among the items submitted nine rhinoceros horns and nine tusks, also ten horses (!) and two elephants. (Müller 1894 Ein Brief: 331–332.)

The Yünnan government also tried to exact tribute from and gave letters of recognition to other states. Its army appeared in 1445 at Bän Mò (Bhamo, Burma) calling for tribute, but was driven off. It reappeared in the following year before Ava, and King Narapati yielded. In 1451 the Yünnan-Chinese government sent the Ava king Narapati "a golden seal as governor of Ava."

old nemesis, Trailōkanāt of Ayuthayā, survived him only by one year and died in 1488.

The sack of Lampāng, 1515

In late 1515 King Rāmathibodī II of Ayuthayā attacked and took Lampāng. The Yuan lost a number of their officers in the battle. It was another of those raids and counter-raids of robbing and abducting people in the border region that took place in these decades.

New walls for Lamphūn and Chiang Mai, 1517

In these times of frequent cross-border raids with probably increased use of fire arms, old-time earth walls and stockades presumably were no longer sufficient to protect a city. New city walls were "invented," their main feature being an earth core with a mantle of brick or laterite work and brick or laterite crenelations on top.

In 1517 Phayā Kāo built such a wall around Lamphūn to protect the stūpa Phra Mahā Thāt Hariphunchai and to stop hostile armies.[45] In the same year he also began a (new) brick wall around Chiang Mai to protect and beautify the city,[46] more than thirty years before Ayuthayā's brick ramparts were built in 1550.

---

45 Most of the considerable remains of the wall were demolished in 1957.
46 The city had a brick wall since about 1345.

Towards the end of Lān Nā's golden age

The end of Lān Nā's golden age announced itself in many little incidents. Soon after 1500 were conducted a number of punitive expeditions or plain raids, mostly unprovoked it seems, into neighboring territories. Ill-conceived and badly executed, they led to the loss of military officers and therefore, since they usually were governors or ministers, to the loss of capable administrators. The many donations of slaves and all their descendants, together with generous annual contributions to monasteries, in the long term perhaps sapped Lān Nā's strength more than the construction of lavish monastery buildings.

3. Everyday Life

Spiritual development was paralleled by material development. If one were to make a basic list of both kinds, one would have to mention:

- A well-organized government bureaucracy; upcountry chief administrators or governors were usually military officers.
- Supraregional and infrastructure facilities such as a network of tracks and unpaved caravan roads, mostly with fords, not bridges, to cross waterways; dams, channels, and huge water-lifting wheels, *luk* หลูก, for irrigation.[47]
- A strong army.

---

47 It is unknown when water lifting wheels were introduced in Lān Nā.

- Skillful craftsmen[48] such as bronze casters and others who were organized according to their specialty in groups (*phuak* พวก) under a chief,[49] and architects or builders.
- Exploitation of natural resources, such as lacquer, resinous oils, and salt.
- Learned monks who wrote books and treatises still famous today.
- A high literacy rate because young men often entered the monkhood for a period of time.
- Poets, musicians, and painters but about whom and their works we know little.
- Medical doctors who divided the range of human maladies into ninety-six illnesses with forty-seven medicines; some local and Indian Ayurvedic-based textbooks have come down to us.
- Good monastic libraries.

---

48 Among other crafts such as lacquerware and stucco decoration, Lān Nā was famous for its bronze Buddha images. In modern popular opinion the oldest and "best" images were made in the remote past at Chiang Sän. That is not corroborated by scholarly findings. The earliest known images are, perhaps, the eight standing and walking bronze repoussé images around the Phra Mahā Thāt, Lamphūn, dating from c. 1330. The oldest known three-dimensional images, dated by their inscriptions, are the four walking and standing images in Wat Phayā Phū and Wat Chāng Kham, Nān, from 1427; and the standing Buddha in Wat Chiang Man, Chiang Mai, from 1465.

49 There were, for instance, the Polers and Paddlers Group, whose members worked on river boats, and the even more specialized Group of the Boatmen of the Queen Mother (*phuak rüa mahā thewī* พวกเรือมหาเทวี).

- Laws and regulations based on old, traditional Thai rules of conduct, on Mon Rācha sāt (*rājaśāstra* ราชศาสตร์) and previous royal decisions, which provided a background of justice with much room for private initiative.
- Moderate taxes and limited unpaid work for government and princes (corvée) who often used the income to donate monastery buildings, Buddha images, and even entire monasteries complete with manpower and a permanent income.

All this made Lān Nā until after 1500 a flourishing community. Monarchs and princes had absolute power but usually consulted extensively with officials and monks, and the ordinary people enjoyed much personal freedom.

Yet, this splendor carried already germs of its future destruction: for instance, a leaning towards individualism and strong local personalities as against state order and a powerful overlord or king; a preference of persons over abstract principles; and lavish spending on "economically unprofitable" projects, mostly religious.

The sangāyana, 1477

Already from about 1330 on, the princes and people had become deeply attracted to Buddhism, and after 1400 there were monks, in particular among the learned forest-dwelling monks or *araññavāsī*, who doubted the purity of the local traditional Buddhism and wished to cleanse it. Monks and even royally sponsored envoys traveled to Ceylon and India to study Buddhism and Buddhist architecture at its root. One of the highlights was in 1477 when a Buddhist council (*sangāyana*) opened in Wat Jet Yòt near Chiang Mai with the aim to purify the canonical scriptures from aberrations. In Thailand, or at least in the north, this is counted as the Eighth Buddhist world council.

Unfortunately, the resultant cleansed text version seems to have been lost. It is thought that the council tried to reestablish an old, local Pāli text tradition that was possibly quite independent of Ceylon and Burma. Traces of such a tradition have been found in several Lān Nā manuscripts.

Construction of religious buildings and images

In this period falls the erection of an astonishing number of large religious buildings and casting of Buddha images. Obviously people were affluent and the "economy" must have flourished. Many monasteries, old ones as well as newly founded ones, received donations for their upkeep in the form of slaves (or rather retainers, bondsmen), land, fixed amounts of annual land-taxes, and fixed amounts of annual contributions such as rice, areca nuts, or salt.

We are very fortunate to know certain details from inscriptions on stone slabs or stone pillars and from inscriptions laid down directly on Buddha images, because such details are completely missing in chronicles. For instance, in 1411 the governor of Phayao, the first to bear the unusual and exalted title of Jao Sī Mün "lord of forty thousand," built a large monastery, Wat Suwanna Mahā Wihān, and founded forty-two filial monasteries for all of which he donated the principal Buddha image. The mother monastery has not yet been identified, but about half a dozen of the filial monasteries are known to still exist as ruins or as active monasteries.

In 1447 the stūpa Phra Mahā Thāt in Lamphūn received its present shape and size. Among other changes, eight over-life-size standing bronze repoussé Buddha images, made in about 1330 and previously probably adorning the stūpa's predecessor, were now attached around the *aṇḍa* or "bell" คอระฆัง of the stūpa. Though they were thickly covered with protective coating and gilding in the last restoration in 1980, they are still faintly visible from below, in particular when the sun is in the right position early in the morning or in late afternoon.

The Jedī Luang in Chiang Mai, begun in about 1391 as a *rājakuṭa* "royal memorial" and several times built over and added to, was enlarged in 1481 to a height of 70–80 meters by the master craftsman Mün Dam Phrā Khot.[50] In 1545, an earthquake caused its upper part to fall down and its southern flank to crumble. The impressive ruin underwent a controversial restoration in 1990–1992.

In 1523 was built, on a plain field about 1 km north of Phayao, Lān Nā's then probably largest Buddha image, Phra Jao Ton Lu-ang or Phra Jao Thung Iang, today the principal Buddha image in Wat Sī Khōm Kham.

In the decades around 1500 were produced by far the greatest number of bronze Buddha images. Lān Nā's oldest known dated image inscribed with *tham* letters was cast in several pieces in 1465; it is a life-size standing image, now in Wat Chiang Man, Chiang

---

50 Mün Dam Phrā Khot หมื่นด้ามพร้าคต also was the master craftsman who cast the big Buddha image Phra Jao Khäng Khom in 1483. The image is now in Wat Sī Köt, Chiang Mai.

Mai. While in Phayao, Prince Yuthisathian founded a monastery whose ruins still exist, Wat Phayā Ruang, and in 1477 deposited in it a newly cast bronze Buddha image with a high gold content. The image is now in Bangkok, in the Phutthaisawan Hall of the National Museum where it is called, after a central Thai fashion, Luang Phò Nāk หลวงพ่อนาก "Great Father of Red Gold." Incidentally, the image has an inscription in which the founder is called, Abhinavabhojarājarājā Yudhiṣṭhirā อภินวโภชราชราชา ยุธิษฐิร.

Powerful Buddha images and palladia

Lān Nā had many Buddha images that were famous for one reason or another. They usually had names hinting at their specialty: Phra Fon Sän Hä พระฝนแสนห่า "Holy (lord) of 100,000 rain showers" would be an image that, if propitiated, could bring rain. Also of other images it was (and is) thought that they will bring rain if carried in a ceremony around the town, for instance the image Phra Jao Thòng Thip พระเจ้าทองทิพย์ "Holy lord with heavenly bronze" of Wat Phra Sing, Chiang Mai, so called because it has a spot of bronze of a different color.

Again other images were supposed by mainly Western authors to be city protectors or state representatives, known as palladia. For instance, it is said that the Phra Phuttha Chinarāt (Jinarāja) was the palladium of Phitsanulōk, that the Sandalwood Image (now disappeared) was the palladium of Phayao, the "Emerald Buddha" (now in Bangkok) the palladium of Chiang Rāi, the Setangkhamani image (in Wat Chiang Man, Chiang Mai) the palladium of Lamphūn, and the black stone Sikhī image (now disappeared) the palladium of Lampāng.

But it seems to me that this idea of a city / country palladium image hardly existed in Lān Nā, if at all. Images were thought to be powerful, but for individual persons, not for the city, state, or country, even if they "belonged" to or were associated with a city. They surely cannot be compared with the classical Greek or Roman palladia.

Non-Buddhist beliefs and practices

Tangible remains of archaic Thai animism and ancestor worship, more and more overlaid or penetrated by Theravāda Buddhism, was the main religion in Lān Nā. In spite of all official attention paid to Buddhism, there was a latent penchant for non-Buddhist beliefs and practices. The case of Phayā Sām Fang Kän has already been mentioned in the last chapter; he venerated all sorts of spirits and items and furthered Buddhism as well. His son, Tilōk, though a fervent Buddhist and patron of the order, even had part of the city wall of Chiang Mai dismantled, a stretch of the moat filled in, the propitious tree of the city felled, after a sorcerer told him that by doing so and building his new palace on that spot, this would fulfill his ambition to become a universal emperor as King Aśoka.

There was a small minority who adhered to Hinduism, perhaps merchants of Indian descent, because near Chiang Mai's Thā Phä Gate, the bronze torso of an Avalokiteśvara image was found, which can be dated to between 1400 and 1500.

Brahmanism, no newcomer, now manifested itself more than before. But, as in Burma, it then and later played a small role if compared to Cambodia's or central Thailand's Brahmanical rituals and practices.

In particular, astronomy or astrology, with a belief in the power of planets and their position, became widespread. Whereas in earlier times such sober documents as inscriptions merely dated and stated what had to be said, they now were accompanied not only by dates which described minute calendrical details such as the *hòrakhun* หรคูณ (haraguṇa),[51] but also by a *duang chatā* ดวงชะตา, a horoscope in the form of a circle divided into twelve sections showing the position of planets in the twelve zodiacal signs. Obviously the exact fixing of an auspicious moment had now become desirable, and also its propagation. The oldest known of such horoscopes is on the already mentioned standing Buddha image of 1465 in Wat Chiang Man, Chiang Mai, followed by horoscopes on stone inscriptions of 1468, 1476, and 1483. Astrology, as medicine, was exercised by specialist monks and laymen.

Perhaps another Brahmanic practice, the still popular *süp chatā* สืบชะตา "life prolonging" ceremony, became now more general.

Knowledge of the Vedasatthas seemingly was accepted as useful but secondary to Buddhism.

Omens were observed, and bones of freshly slaughtered chickens were studied to foretell future events, such as the outcome of a battle. However, that may not have been a newly acquired part of Brahmanic science but could have been practiced by the Yuan since earlier times because the Chinese also used bone oracles.

---

51 The Haraguṇa (Ahargaṇa) indicates the number of days from the beginning of the era (Culasakkarāja) until the date in question.

Religious literature

Many of the important learned Lān Nā writings seem to date from this period, as far as we can know and date them. They all are religious or religion-related works of the Buddhist Theravāda school, even those that today we would rather classify as historical accounts. Monks had at their disposal well-stocked libraries, probably even filled with the old classical religious commentaries from Ceylon, which were later lost.

Here only a few shall be named. Some Brahmanical and related literature probably existed as well. However, no original manuscript of these classical works have reached us. We only have copies of copies at an unknown number of removals from the original.

Between about 1450 and 1500 the redaction, in Pāli, took place, of a Phra Mālai พระมาลัย text (Mālaya Sutta) and of a commentary (ṭika) on it. It is a tale of the saintly monk Phra Mālai and his visits to heaven and hell. That was, however, not a completely new composition but a development or adaptation from older texts which originally derived from Lanka.

In 1516 the monk Ratanapañña รตนปญฺญ of Chiang Mai completed the first part of his chronicle Jinakālamālī ชินกาลมาลี "A garland of epochs of the conqueror," or in modern language, "Sequence of events in Buddhism." It was written in Pāli and is the history of the Wat Pā Däng monks (Sīhaḷabhikkhus, New Sinhalese Sect). This chronicle was at least once updated and continued until 1527. It is one of Chiang Mai's and Lān Nā's best chronicles.

In 1520 the monk Sirimaṅgala สิริมํคล of Chiang Mai composed, in Pāli, his Cakkavāḷadīpanī จกฺกวาฬทีปนี "Illustration of the universe," a cosmological and consmogonical treatise on the world systems according to the Buddhist Theravāda view. The oldest known copy is dated 1538 with a slightly different title: Cakkavāḷatthadīpanī จกฺกวาฬตฺทฺทีบนี. Based on its age it could be a copy made directly from the original and thus is probably the manuscript copy closest to any of the classical works.

In 1524 Sirimaṅgala wrote his Mangala(ttha)dipanī มังคล(ตฺถ)ทีปนี "Illustrator of the Meaning of the Maṅgalasuttanta" in Pāli, a commentary on the Mangalasutta in the Tipiṭaka.

Possibly also the oldest recension of the Paṭhamasambodhi ปฐมสํโพธิ, a tale of the life of the Buddha, was composed in this period in Chiang Mai.

Secular literature

In the field of secular literature, there were juridical, medical, and other textbooks, but we seem to know little about belles-lettres. Perhaps much was still oral. We know that people were fond of rhymes because some of the official stone inscriptions were partly or even wholly written in rhyme or regularly accented prose, such as *kham ham* คำฮ่ำ (คำร่ำ), also called *kham rāi bōrān* คำ ร่ายโบราณ, or *lam nam* ลำนำ. Surely there were folktales of the kind that are being told even now, touching on the universe and nature (sun, moon, stars, animals, rivers, etc.), didactic stories, romances, stories of clever stupid fools, spirit and ghost tales, and riddles.

Only copies of copies of these works seem to have survived. The oldest preserved Lān Nā manuscript is dated only 1471. A particularly distressing case is the Jinakālamālī. Of this important chronicle not even one copy seems to have survived in Lān Nā;

the known or reported manuscripts are in Bangkok, Phnom Penh and Sri Lanka.

Only a few of these Lān Nā works indicate the date of their composition and the name of the author; the copies, however, in many cases name the scribe, the date on which the copy was finished, and the name of the person who sponsored the copying including the price. Copying of religious texts was a very merit-gaining act.

Some works that at present are often considered old, in reality were written only in the recent past though probably after oral sources, i.e. traditional tales. That error came about because many if not most of these works purport to be or seem to be "chronicles" of the most remote past, often long before the time of Mang Rāi. They are not precisely fakes since they were not intended to deceive; they are better called myth-chronicles or pseudo-chronicles, or simply historical legends. They are often characterized by: (1) supernatural events (the real chronicles are very much matter-of-fact), such as the arrival of god Indra, of a Buddha, or of a monk from the Buddha's circle; (2) by the use of words not usual in old Lān Nā (which marks these legends as imports, mostly, it seems, from the Burmese Shan States, from Laos, and from central Thailand); and (3) by great efforts to explain the meaning of local toponyms—why this hill has this name, etc., usually because of such and such (supernatural) event which allegedly took place there.

These works may originally have been local or imported myths and legends, remembrances of once real happenings, which for a long time had been orally transmitted, had been changed in the process, and which in modern times, after 1800 or even after 1900, were written down and, at the end of the old legend, received a continuation, a second part, which continued them with more recent historical material to form a myth-chronicle. Thus, the beginning is a legend, and the end is fairly historical. An example is the chronicle of Chiang Sän whose unknown compiler covers the entire period from Lāo Jong down to the year 1905.

Relations with the outside

Although there was frequently some kind of warfare between Lān Nā and central Thailand, it did not hinder intensive commercial and religious interchange between the two regions.

Among the thousands of people that in 1451 followed Prince Yuthisathian from Phitsanulōk to Phayao surely were numerous artisans of all sorts. At the time, Phitsanulōk was the center of the so-called post-classic Sukhōdayan school of sculpture. They must have included carpenters, masons, weavers, potters, wood carvers, bronze casters, gilders and jewelers, painters, and calligraphers. When Sangkhalōk was part of Lān Nā from c. 1460 until 1475, probably more came up to Lān Nā. But the inverse probably happened also. There are definite traces of Lān Nā art in the northern parts of the old Sukhōthai empire, and it is now commonly assumed that most of them date from this period.

Lān Nā also maintained an exchange of ideas and commercial goods with her other neighbors, and here again she was an importer as well as an exporter. The Burmese, for instance, took over from the Yuan a certain type of lacquered container that is still called yun in Burma. Lān Nā took over, presumably from the

Lamphūn Mon, a type of standing Buddha image, and "exported" it to Sukhōthai. Chiang Mai disseminated, or "exported," her purified Buddhism to Chiang Tung, Chiang Rung, and Luang Phra Bāng. On the other hand, the radiating arch, typical for Lān Nā but hardly used by other Thai groups, reached Lān Nā probably from Burma. Chinese artists, presumably from Yünnan, either worked themselves in Lān Nā or they had Thai Yuan pupils.[52]

Lān Nā people went abroad for study and for making merit, as has been mentioned, but foreigners also came here for similar purposes. Visitors from central Thailand, Laos, Burma, and Ceylon were common. The visitor from the most remote country on record came from Tibet, albeit after Lān Nā's golden age had passed. The Tibetan monk Taranatha wrote in the sixteenth century that his spiritual teacher, Buddhagupta, had traveled to Haripunja, i.e. to Lamphūn and Chiang Mai.

As for certain features of popular Buddhism such as fictitious travels of the Buddha in Lān Nā and beyond, and the existence of Buddha relics and Buddha footprints here, Burma with the Shan States and Lān Nā presumably inspired each other based on traditions from Lanka (Ceylon). For example, it seems that the background of the legend which tells about the origin of the holy site and stūpa Phra Thāt Dòi Tung (50 km north of Chiang Rāi)

---

52 An example is the cave monastery Wat Umōng at the foot of Dòi Suthep beyond the Chiang Mai airport. The vaults are built with the radiating arch. Its wall paintings, now largely hidden under layers of sinter, show Chinese influence. The monastery was built in stages between c. 1380–1520.

derived from Lanka via Müang Yòng in the Shan States, perhaps in the decades around 1400.

Lān Nā owed by far the greatest spiritual debt to Lanka, which was regarded as the upholder of unadulterated Buddhism. The so-called Burmese monasteries in Lān Nā date back only to between c. 1850 and 1900 when Burmese merchants in Lān Nā, chiefly under British protection, became wealthy in the wood and timber trade and wished to make merit.

The monastery

Religious life, and to a wide extent social life, was centered around a monastery or *wat* วัด. The monastery was of primary importance in everyday life. Many villages had their own mon-astery; larger settlements and towns had several.

The main building was the *wihān* วิหาร (P. *vihāra*), usually built on a rectangular plan, the main door in the east, with an altar at the west wall on which was the larger than life-size main Bud-dha image, *phra prathān* พระประธาน, facing east. The *wihān* was the main assembly hall, used for religious and secular gatherings; travelers could sleep here.

At a short distance behind the *wihān*, i.e. west of it, stood a *jedī* เจดีย์ (*cetiya*, stūpa), often encased in a sheathing of *thòng jangkō* ทองจังโก plates, a costly bronze alloy that contained gold, frequently gilded. A *jedī* would shelter a relic, sometimes thought to be of the Buddha and brought from India, enshrined either in a crypt below or in a little chamber further up in the *jedī*. For that reason the entire *jedī* structure was colloquially called (*phra*) *thāt* (พระ)ธาตุ (P. *dhātu* "relic"). It was a reliquary.

The monks lived in one or several houses called *kutī* กุฏิ (*kuṭī),*
often to the south of the *wihān.*

Only some monasteries had a small, specially consecrated plot
of land, the *uposatha* premises, which was marked by eight *sīmā*
or boundary stones, and on which stood the *bōt* or *ubōsot* (P.
uposathāgāra), a building of modest size compared to the *wihān;*
it was not open to the public and was never entered by women. It
served only for the most sacred religious acts, *sangkha kam* สังฆกรรม
(P. *sanghakamma*), such as the ordination of new monks (age
twenty and over) or the bi-monthly *uposatha* reunion, *ubosatha
kam* อุโบสถกรรม (P. *uposathakamma*) on the days of the full and
new moon, part of which was (and is) the recital of the 227 rules
governing the life of monks (P. *paṭimokkha*).

Larger monasteries or even little ones with a scholarly-minded
abbot sometimes had enormous collections of books, i.e. writings
on palm leaves, *bai lān* ใบลาน, arranged in bundles or fascicles,
phūk ผูก. They were kept in the library called *hò tham* หอธรรม
"Dhamma hall" (P. *Dhamma*, here "Buddhist instructive literature, scriptures") or *hò trai* หอไตร (Traipiṭaka, Tipiṭaka). This was
a separate building that was sometimes built on posts standing in
a pond, or at least the book chamber was on the second floor, to
discourage white ants. In the library, the book bundles were kept
wrapped in cloth with an inscribed wooden marker that indicated
the title. These book bundles were placed in large, black-and red
lacquered wooden boxes with a lid, *hīp tham* หีบธรรม "scripture
boxes." Monastery libraries mostly held religious writings, but also
historical, medical, and other secular books because monasteries
were the centers of learning, knowledge, and teaching.

Though monks went out in the early morning, as soon as the lines in the palm of the hand could be distinguished, to collect their alms-food (*binthabāt* บิณฑบาต, P. *piṇḍapāta*), a monastery also had a kitchen-house in which servants or slaves prepared their own food and food for monks in case alms-food was not enough. A drum tower, a well, a bathing-house, a toilet-house, and other utilitarian buildings like storage rooms and even stables, often also a bodhi tree, completed the monastery complex which was surrounded by a wall. Unlike in central Thailand, the monastery did not have a crematory because the dead were cremated outside the village or town on a special cremation ground. Burying corpses, especially those who had died from an accident or were poor or living far out, was also practiced. It seems that cremation became more general only in fairly recent times.

Wihān and *ubōsot* had an architecture different from the other buildings which were raised on posts like the usual Yuan houses: they were built on a low, solid base, often were made of bricks or laterite blocks, and had gracefully curved tiered roofs with low eaves, quite different in aspect from the high-roofed monastic buildings in central Thailand. Gables of *bōt* and *wihān* also had wind boards or wind breakers (here called *bai rakā* ใบระกา) but they were richly sculpted and did not cross; they ended at the top of the gable from which projected a sculpted piece of wood, *chò fā* ช่อฟ้า, often reminiscent of the head and part of the body of a big bird or the trunk of an elephant. Presumably for these large buildings big iron nails, *lek luā* เหล็กหลวา," were used to help hold the timber, as it is attested for one century later.[53]

While certain architectural features are typical for Lān Nā, they are not absolutely unique. For instance, religious buildings with a tiered roof are also known from far-distant Norway (staff church, Stabskirche). In Bavaria and neighboring Austria, and also in the Spreewald in eastern Germany, many a farmer's or forester's house had crossed ornamented gable boards, called *kalä* in Thai. In Bavaria the ornament may mostly resemble a horse or deer, but it is a serpent head with a little crown in the Spreewald. Perhaps similar architectural requirements led to similar solutions.

Founding a monastery, or adding to an existing one, was perceived as a source of great merit towards a favorable future rebirth. Such merit-making (*tham bun* ทำบุญ, P. *puñña*) included donations (*kap* กับปี < *kanlapanā* กัลปนา," P. *kalapanā*) of fields or plantations, of one's own house and garden (a house could be dismantled and reerected elsewhere with relative ease), of slaves (sometimes a man would even donate himself or his wife and children), and of copies of religious texts, in particular parts of the holy canon (Tipiṭaka), in order to replace worn-out manuscripts.

Monasteries were divided into two groups depending on whether they were located within or very close to a settlement, or at a greater distance from it. The monks of the first group were called city-dwellers (P. *nagaravāsī),* and those of the second group, which was less numerous, forest-dwellers (P. *araññavāsī*). In order

---

53 In 1585, for the rebuilding of the main *wihān* of a major monastery, an amount of 120 kg of nails, *lek luā,* were used.

to qualify as a forest-dweller, a monk had to live, in theory, at least five hundred bow-lengths from the nearest habitation, about one half or one kilometer.

Monks, according to the doctrine, had withdrawn from worldly affairs to devote themselves to studies, mental exercises, and a way of life which, in orthodox Buddhist tradition as exemplified in famous Ceylonese (Sri Lanka) monasteries, would lead them, through future rebirths, to final extinction in *nibbāna*. Part of the effort was to exercise compassion (P. *mettā*). For example, they had to give others an opportunity "to make merit," *tham bun*, by offering alms-food to monks or by making donations to the religion, so that the others too increased their store of merit.

Monks did not do manual work like plowing or even gardening in order to avoid taking animal life unintentionally, nor did they work otherwise actively for their livelihood; such activities fell to the lay sponsors, personal slaves, and servants. But often monks had particular skills, for instance in the arts, among which was counted building and architecture, or in giving advice, and applied them as another form of spreading compassion, or as *tham bun* in general. A village or town with such "good" monks thought (and still thinks) of itself as spiritually strong and quite secure against worldly and supernatural peril.

Monasteries and their accumulated treasures served as banks: a person could borrow money from a monastery. Upon default, he or she became a so-called money-slave, *khon ngön* คนเงิน, of the monastery until the debt was cleared. Being a monastery slave was better than a tax shelter: the person was exempt from taxes and also from corvée labor.

There was yet another category of slaves: those who freely attached themselves to a certain monastery or holy place and pledged to take care of a certain part or a certain building or Buddha image, which was considered an honor. Important monasteries would have more than a hundred of these "honorary slaves."

The Lān Nā house

The typical Lān Nā house, *hüan* (modern Thai *rüan* เรือน "house"), had an open, partly covered porch in front of it and the whole rested on a kind of platform built on stout posts, preferably insect-resistant teak logs, 160–180 cm above the ground. From below, stairs or a removable ladder led up to the uncovered part of the platform.

There were two basic types of houses with similar architecture but made of two different kinds of materials. These were the less expensive and less durable *hüan mai bua* เฮือนไม้บั่ว "bamboo house," whose individual pieces were held together chiefly by twisted slip of bamboo or cane, and the solid wooden house *hüan mai sakat* เฮือนไม้สกัด, whose timbers were joined mainly by tenon and mortise. No iron nails were used, only wooden pegs.

The house had "walls" of bamboo matting or of teak to enclose the sleeping room(s) which could be entered through a door over which was a carved wooden panel, *ham yon* หำยน "magic testicles," that fended off evil and ensured prosperity. Beneath the façade, or gable-end of the house, was a verandah without sidewalls; it was sheltered from sun and rain by the roof. This verandah, *tön* เติ๋น, served as a place to eat meals, receive guests, to do various household chores, and in general was the "social spot" of the house. In front of the verandah, on a level 10–15 cm lower, was an open porch or terrace that was used for various purposes. The whole house, verandah, and terrace, were a tall man's height above the ground, as has been said. The space under the platform served as a storage and working area, also as a shelter for domestic animals.

For windows, the house had either simple, top-hinged hatches that could be pushed open for light and fresh air with a stick, or else sliding or side-hinged shutters, and had a roof of leaves, grass, wooden tiles, or, more recently, baked tiles.

Two wooden planks (or pieces of bamboo split in half length-wise) along the gables served as windbreakers to fix and to protect the roofing material; they crossed each other at the gable top and continued into the air forming a V. These free-standing gable-boards, *kā lä* กาแล "glancing crow" or *kalä* กะแล, were often artfully carved. At present they still are a typical feature of a Lān Nā house though now they are added more as an ornament than for a practical function.

The sidewalls of the house were inclined outwards from the floor to the roof, not inward as in central Thailand. Usually two of these houses stood side by side on the raised platform, the eves close or even touching, with a narrow pathway in between, their façades facing the common terrace. Living here were close relatives, grown children, often the daughter and her husband because marriages were matrilocal, i.e. the groom went to live with his bride at least for some time.

Whether farmhouse or townhouse, it was not complete without a separate kitchen house at the back, on the same level as, and accessible from, the terrace and verandah. It often included a private well, because Thai Yuan prefer water from a well over water from the river and do not use rainwater, as well as a rice granary, and a sheltered rice pounder, *mòng* มอง. The latter consisted of a hollowed-out log into which fell a wooden pestle that a woman operated with her foot by means of a well-balanced lever. The rice was of the glutinous variety, often called "sticky rice" by Westerners, and was steamed *nüng* in an ingenious rice-steamer, hence its local name *khao nüng* เข้าหนึ้ง "steamed rice." But they also ate sesame and millet. Salt, produced from underground brine wells or surface sediments of underlying rock salt, was a common luxury. Non-distilled and distilled alcoholic drinks, *miang* เมี่ยง quid (fermented wild tea leaves with salt), and betel quid (*māk*, i.e. arecanut, betel leaf, and lime) were the usual stimulants.

Most farmers were also fishermen or were skilled in one craft or another. Their houses were similar and a village looked quite uniform.

Washing, bathing, and laundry were done at the brook or river nearby, or with water drawn from the village well, or the private well. Monasteries had latrines made of a stone slab with a hole and underlying cesspool for stool while a groove in the stone slab conducted the urine to the front into the earth, thus neatly separating stool from urine. We know nothing about the toilets in laymen's houses in town. In villages, particular reserved spots in certain groves were in use up until the recent past.

Village, town, and country

Lān Nā was not one single country. It consisted of several countries much as a modern country can be composed of partly

self-governing provinces or states. The basic unit was a settlement called *bān* บ้าน "hamlet, village" (modern Thai "house"),
often a cluster of houses belonging to one family. The leader of
the village was the senior relative or someone else locally chosen.
A number of villages formed a district, *pan nā* ปันนา "one thousand paddy fields." An important village could be fortified with
a rampart and a moat; such a settlement was called a *wiang* เวียง
"town." If a town was inhabited by senior royalty, the *wiang* was
called a *chiang* เชียง "city." Several *bān* with a *wiang* or a *chiang*
formed a *müang* เมือง "country; city-state" (modern Thai "town,
city, country").

A *müang* was an area bordered by hills. Beyond the hills would
be another *müang*. A practical result of such delimitation was that
a *müang* frequently corresponded to (part of) a water-catchment
area and rarely transcended it. The old system of state administration by *müang* to a certain extent was therefore an administration
by watersheds.

A *wiang* typically was located on a little hill close to the moun-
tains surrounding a major valley. The highest point of the hill
would be approximately the middle of the *wiang*. It often had
a triple rampart with dry moats on the slope, not at the foot of
the hill. Sometimes several fortified hills were interconnected by
two rows of ramparts and moats so that the town consisted of
two or more compartments. A new compartment could also be
added by simply enclosing a plot of land outside the old rampart.
The principle of building compartment towns later was largely
abandoned but never quite disappeared. Even Chiang Mai, with
its square layout in a flat area, had a compartment added to it as

late as in the decades after 1550, by the so-called *kamphäng din* กำแพงดิน "earth wall" in the east and south.

Government and country administration

The king (*phayā, phanyā* พญา),[54] advised by selected monks and laymen, also by astrologers, officially exercised his power from a throne, *thän käo* แท่นแก้ว.[55] He ruled the country through a bureaucracy of appointed officials who were ranked in a numeric command scale. The lowest rank was *nāi hā* นายห้า "chief of five." The next higher ranks were chief of 10, 50, 100, 1,000, 10,000, and 100,000. From 1,000 on up, the official was no longer addressed as *nāi* but as *jao* เจ้า "lord, prince." In earlier times these figures probably indicated power of command over groups of people but in Lān Nā's golden age they merely denoted rank in government service. The minister of records, for instance, had the title *mün nangsü* หมื่นหนังสือ "(Mr.) Ten Thousand, (of the Ministry of) Documents." The title *sän* แสน "100,000" was rare and usually was reserved for positions of a more ceremonial role. The real power was with the *jao mün* "prince of ten thousand" who governed key city-states such as Lampāng, Chiang Sän, or Fāng. Above all of them was the king who was beyond any num-

---

54 Not to be confused with the central Thai word *phrayā* พระยา, title of a high government official. The Lān Nā title *phayā* was later "devalued" until in the nineteenth century it only denoted a minor official, village head, then often pronounced "*phiyā.*"

55 The same word is used for "altar," the elevated dais for the main Buddha image in a *wihān*.

ber and who in theory owned all land[56] and could give orders to any person. Female administrators were not unknown and in the sixteenth century there were even two ruling queens.

Incidentally, for official royal progress or while traveling through rough country, the king and other dignitaries would ride on elephants. However, for swift transport, road permitting, he would ride a horse.[57]

Government work was carried out through appointed officials who could be rotated to other places, for instance governors of city-states, but local day-to-day administration was in the hands of locally chosen persons such as village chiefs, irrigation directors, and monastery lay administrators. Important issues were sent up through channels to higher levels for decision. A key matter such as the delimiting of *uposatha* premises which involved the formal donation by the king of a plot of land to the Buddhist order, *sangha*, and approval of the planting of *sīmā* stones, had to go all the way up to the royal court where it was processed and from where it was returned through the proper channels to the

---

56 In practical life, anybody could go and clear a plot of land and begin farming it. As long as he farmed the land and paid rent or tax, it belonged to him de facto, even if the plot of land was not his property; he could buy and sell only his right to a plot, not the plot itself. Land tenure thus was based on using it, on usufruct, not on title.

Taxes were paid in kind or in cash, were based on the type of land and on the kind of crops planted, and were payable to local administrators who had their own arrangements with higher authority and, ultimately, the Crown.

57 For instance, when in 1441 Phayā Sām Fang Kän fled from his burning palace in Wiang Jet Lin at the foot of Dòi Suthep, he rode on a horse to his palace in Chiang Mai town.

DECLINE AND LOSS OF INDEPENDENCE

place of origin. Major decisions were officially engraved on stone tablets or square stone pillars and the inscribed stones (*silā jārük* ศิลาจารึก) were placed in public view at the locality concerned. These stone inscriptions, usually written in the secular, official Fak Khām script and in Yuan dialect, precisely dated and often accompanied, at the top, by an engraved round chart, or horoscope (*duang chatā* ดวงชะตา) indicating the planets' position, are unique historical documents. Most of them are now kept in museums.

The Lawa

The autochthonous Lawa were not "integrated." They preferred to live together in Lawa villages, mostly near the foot of the hills and in the lower valleys. But they did not keep apart, either. Numbers of them lived with or near Thais. Lawa men and women were monastery servants or participated in monastery services the same as Thais. Some Lawa men were monks and later, on leaving the order, became respected laymen. Lawa villages had their own administrators but came under the overall administrative bureaucracy of the country. They often enjoyed special rights, for instance being exempt from corvée, but had special duties, for instance supplying iron or other particular materials.

Decline and Loss of Independence
1526–1558

A general decline slowly began in the years after 1500 and soon became serious after the death of Phayā Käo in 1526. The decline had multiple causes, some long-standing and others more recent, so that several factors combined to end Lān Nā's independence for good. One was a lessening of the king's control over certain matters, in part being the result of administrative decisions already made during the time of Phayā Tilok (1441–1487) when a top official demanded, and received, increased power. Another was growing internal strife. Foreign relations might have been handled better. Perhaps the most serious of all were certain financial actions influencing the economy.

It may be thought that old-time economy was something simple and rather stable, that price increases were caused only by perhaps a one-time bad harvest, automatically rectified in the following year. In the case of Chiang Mai, however, it is probable that costly secular and religious projects burdened the royal treasury and the population alike, and there is even the possibility of financial manipulation[58] by one or two kings who needed money; only in the years around 1517 had both Chiang Mai and Lamphūn received new brick and laterite walls, and in the years around 1520, Wat Pā Däng near Chiang Mai had been lavishly renovated, to name only three enterprises. Other possible causes were the considerable number of slaves as well as the amount of real estate and taxes donated to monasteries and thus, at least in part, unavailable for the "national economy." Within about thirty years, there seems to have occurred a rising of prices, an inflation of over 40 percent,

---

58 It seems that when the king paid contractors, instead of giving 100 monetary units, he paid out only 80 and decreed that these 80 should be valued as 100.

which must have been a serious problem for a "national economy" that was mainly based on agriculture for local consumption but not without an "industry" and internal and external trade. People at the time did not at all grasp what happened to the "value of their money" and thought that the spirits were angry or that the conjunction of the stars was not good.

There was corresponding disorder in the political field. During the twenty-five years following the death of Phayā Käo, six rulers in succession mounted the throne of Chiang Mai; besides, the country was without a ruler for four years because no agreement in the choice of a new king could be reached; and none of the six rulers ended his reign peacefully: they were either murdered, or deposed, or they abdicated.

Lān Nā became weakened to such an extent that her condition invited invasion from Burma. When the well-organized and, at the time, expansionist Burmese attacked Chiang Mai in 1558 under some pretext, funds were exhausted, people were disinclined to fight, and the city surrendered practically without opposition. Soon after, the whole of Lān Nā was in Burmese hands

Fragmentation, 1558–1775

The Burmese were not overly harsh masters, at least in the beginning, and also later, when tensions rose to a permanently simmering rebellion that erupted frequently, there were Burmese officials with whom the Yuan were content. In 1565, the Burmese military commander of Chiang Mai had a huge bronze Buddha image cast, under participation of the Chiang Mai royalty; it was called Buddha Müang Rāi พระพุทธเมืองราย, obviously in memory of Phayā Mang Rāi. The image still exists in Wat Chai Phra Kiat. It is of pure Yuan style and exemplifies the observation that the Burmese occupation of Lān Nā had no or very little influence on the art of Lān Nā.

Lān Nā's status was at first that of an occupied vassal kingdom with Burmese garrisons and Burmese administrators in key positions. Some of the latter actually were Thais, either from Lān Nā or from the neighboring Shan States. Until 1578, when the dynasty of Phayā Mang Rāi possibly became extinct, the Burmese allowed Yuan princes on the throne of Chiang Mai; thereafter, they sent several of their own royal princes; later, they appointed or confirmed the princes of the various *müang* who often belonged to an old local ruling family.

The more important Lān Nā city-states now had a tripartite government. Nominally at the top was the ruling prince, called *phayā* พญา or *jao fā* เจ้าฟ้า. His authority was limited. Next came the Burmese resident or governor, *myowun*, who held the real civilian power. The third was the military commander of the town, *sitke* (often called *jakkai*, among other terms, in Yuan texts). But many times Burmese power was represented only by a *myowun* or a *sitke*.

Traders and monks from neighboring countries had been and, at the beginning of the Burmese occupation, still were frequent visitors in Lān Nā but the occidental world knew little about it. For centuries it was believed and shown on maps that the Mä Nam Jao Phrayā, Bangkok's river (Menam), through its upper section, Chiang Mai's Mä Ping River, originated in a big lake near Chiang

Mai, and the Portuguese poet Camões (1525–1580) even mentioned the "fact" in one of his works. Few Westerners ventured this far inland, not so much, it seems, because of local hostility, but because of physical travel and transportation difficulties. Even the name of the principal city-state Chiang Mai was not known for certain; there probably were more than fifty different ways of spelling it, representing various forms of the name under which the city was known to its neighbors.[59]

The first Westerner on record to reach Chiang Mai was the London merchant Ralph Fitch who visited here in the last months of 1587: "I went from Pegu to Jamahey (Chiang Mai) . . . , it is five and twenty days journey Northeast from Pegu . . . Jamahey is a very fair and great town, with fair houses of stone, well peopled, and the streets are very large, the men very well set and strong, with a cloth about them, bare-headed and bare-footed, for in all these countries they wear no shoes. The women be much fairer than those of Pegu . . . Hither to Jamahey come many merchants out of China and bring great store of musk, gold, silver and many other things of China work. Here is great store of victuals . . . (and) of copper and benjamin . . ."[60] Fitch must have witnessed

---

59 One of these, not immediately recognizable, is *Zimmé*—in the nineteenth century, a frequent English rendering of the Burmese pronunciation. The modern official form is *Chiang Mai*.

60 Ralph Fitch, "The Voyage of Master Ralph Fitch . . ." In *Purchas His Pilgrims*, London / Glasgow, 1905, Vol. 2, 194f. I have modernized the orthography. 'Benjamin' is the fragrant gum-resin of *Styrax benzoides*, the *kamyān* tree ต้นกำยาน, used medicinally and for food conservation. Lān Nā (and Siam) was among the chief benzoin producing regions.

the last vestiges of Lān Nā's golden age, when it was already in Burmese hands, soon to be ravaged by endless civil wars.

The first known Western merchant to actually trade here was another Englishman, Thomas Samuel, whom the East India Company sent to Chiang Mai in 1613 with cloth goods of 2,025 ticals value. He had sold part of his cloth and sent an assistant to Ayuthayā with 2,456 ticals when he was captured in 1614 by the army of the Burmese king coming from Pegu which again seized Chiang Mai in that year; he later died in Burma.

The trade expectations of the British were also expressed in a letter by British captain William Eaton who wrote in 1617 to the East India Company: ". . . if the trade of Jangamay (Chiang Mai) be once opened, which will be this next year it is thought. It is a place that will vent (buy) much clothing, as I am given to understand for great profit, as six or seven of one, besides the returns that may be made from thence, which is gold, rubies, and other precious stones; as also benjamin, sealing wax, which commodities are in great request at the Coast of Coromandel, besides deer skins which are there very cheap. This place of Jangama is now under the King of Pegew (Pegu, Burma) who has gotten it by wars from the King of Siam." From the context it is apparent that "clothing" here means "India cloth, and likewise other clothes that comes from the Coast of Coromandel."[61]

---

61 Reginald le May, *An Asian Arcady*, Cambridge, 1926; reprint Bangkok: White Lotus, 1986, 44. Sealing wax was obtained from *kh(r)ang*, sticklac (lac), the excretion of an insect which lives on the twigs of certain trees and sucks sap from the bark; sticklac could also be made into shellac for polish; from about 1890 on, it again became a valued export item when shellac was used in the

But Samuel's fate and the following unsafe times delayed efforts to open up the land to Western trade for nearly 250 years, until about 1860, well after the Burmese had left for good.

From about 1600 on, the Yuan made great efforts towards self-liberation but because of internal disunity could not achieve lasting results. There were also attacks or intervention from the outside. For instance, in the years around 1600 King Naresuan of Ayuthayā brought Chiang Mai under his influence and in 1662 King Nārāi occupied Chiang Mai. In each case, the Burmese recaptured the town after some time. If a Burmese official was well liked, Yuan would side with Burmese and fight Siamese, Laotians, or other Yuan. These repeated efforts at self-liberation and short-lived alliances, many still incompletely known, accumulated to about two hundred years of intermittent warfare within Lān Nā which ruined the country economically and culturally. Food production and production of all other kinds of goods and articles decreased dramatically. The huge population shifts and the desertion and decay of many of Lān Nā's formerly splendid towns date from that period.

Between 1701 and 1733, the Burmese divided the country into what may be called "East Lān Nā" and "West Lān Nā" in order to better deal with insurrections. "East Lān Nā" had as capital Chiang Sän (a city the Burmese favored over Chiang Rāi) and was practically annexed because it was placed, with Nān, Phrä, and Lampang and their dependencies, directly under administra-

---

production of gramophone records. As for the rubies, most of them probably were imported from Burma (Mogok ruby mines).

tion from the Burmese capital Ava. Chiang Mai and the western principalities continued as a military-controlled vassal state.

By now, Lān Nā, impoverished and fractured, and Burma, in the meantime also grown weaker but militarily still powerful, had reached a stalemate where Burma could no longer actively control Lān Nā and the latter could not extricate itself from under the Burmese.

Only after the Burmese had devastated Ayuthayā in 1767 did some far-seeing princes and military men in Lān Nā (Prince Kāwila เจ้ากาวิละ and the Chiang Mai governor, Phayā Jā Bān Bun Mā พญาจ่าบ้าน บุญมา) and in central Thailand (King Tāk Sin and generals Surasī and Jakrī [Chakri], the future King Rama I) realize that they had to combine their resources in order to overcome the Burmese. Reversing a centuries-old policy, Lān Nā princes now agreed to place themselves under the king of Siam. The idea for this new policy seemingly originated in Lān Nā. Though no protocol of the agreements is known, later events show to what the two sides consented: the major Lān Nā princes, for instance the ruler of Chiang Mai, would become direct vassal kings of the king of Siam while keeping their own vassals; each vassal would be independent in the interior administration of his territory and his vassals; the vassal would guard Siam's northern borders; Siam would send military assistance if the vassal was attacked; the immediate objective in the north would be the recapture of Chiang Mai. This new policy, and strategy, was soon successful. A joint Thai-Thai army, Yuan and Siamese, seized Chiang Mai from the Burmese, probably in the night from Saturday to Sunday, 14–15 January 1775.

Renaissance and Integration as a Part of Siam / Thailand, c. 1775–present

The recapture of Chiang Mai from the Burmese in 1775 was the first step of a long struggle of twenty-nine years to push the Burmese out. Their last stronghold, Chiang Sän, was retaken only in 1804. It was likewise the beginning of Lān Nā's renaissance and also of its integration in Siam (called Thailand since 1939).

King Tāk Sin immediately nominated the new rulers of the three liberated cities. For Chiang Mai, he appointed Phrayā Jā Bān with the new title Phrayā Wichian Prakān; for Lampāng, Phrayā Kāwila, and for Lamphūn, the former ruler Sitke Khäng with the new title Phrayā Wai Wongsā. It so happened that at the time when Chiang Mai was seized, Jao Nòi Withūn, a high Nān aristocrat, was in Burmese service in Chiang Mai; he was the son of a previous Nān ruler. King Tāk Sin made him vassal ruler of Nān on the same occasion.

Lān Nā thus did not join Siam as an entity, but as different principalities that formed an eastern group with Nān as the leader and a western group with Chiang Mai as the leader. But this time Chiang Sän, Chiang Rāi, and Lampāng were part of the western group.

The Chiang Mai royal court lived from 1775 until 1797 in a camp near Pā Sāng south of Lamphūn. This was for military reasons because the city had suffered much physical damage and a serious loss of population along with a loss of food supply. During this time, Chiang Mai was nearly deserted. After King Kāwila had ceremoniously reentered the city on Thursday, 9 March

1797, Chiang Mai received new fortifications. What is still left of fortifications at present dates from that period around 1800.

Nān had likewise been abandoned for many years, since about 1776. Only in 1802 did the vassal king of Nān, Jao Attha Wòra Pannyō, move his court back into the old city.

Until about 1800, the Burmese kept reattacking Chiang Mai and other towns, tenaciously defended by the Yuan; time and again the Siamese sent an army to help out. Very slowly, the country was wrested back from the Burmese and from local warlords, necessitating innumerable campaigns, some of them into the Shan States. These campaigns not only served to secure borders but also helped towards solving the pressing problem of a lack of population, caused by the events of the past. The scattered population had to be brought back, and until well after 1800 their numbers were occasionally augmented by forced settlement in Lān Nā of people from the Shan States. Yet, there were not enough people to fill all empty towns. Fāng and even Phayao were depopulated. Settlers from Chiang Mai, Lamphūn, and Lampāng had to be sent out to resettle at least Chiang Rāi and Chiang Sän. Chiang Rāi was officially refounded in 1844, on which occasion the size of the walled town was approximately doubled.

The northern city-states which had placed themselves under Bangkok were independent as far as their inner administration was concerned. But they were not allowed to negotiate with foreign powers, and their rulers, vassal kings, or princes had to be officially nominated by their overlord, the king of Siam. The rulers were required to bring at fixed intervals, usually every three years, token tribute consisting chiefly of stylized gold and silver trees, and they had to present themselves regularly at the royal court in Bangkok. The latter was no particular hardship since life in the capital was interesting and the shopping was good.

Between 1804 and 1810, in the course of Lān Nā's efforts to regain former territory and areas of influence lost to the Burmese in the north, Chiang Tung (Kengtung) and her eastern and southern dependencies Möng (Müang) Yāng, Möng Yòng, etc., became tributary to Bangkok through Chiang Mai. However, they later withdrew for reasons of their own and also under pressure from Burma.

Soon afterwards, between 1850 and 1854, Chiang Rung (Chiang Hung, Cheli) in Yünnan's southern region of Sip-Sòng Pan Nā, in the past, like Chiang Tung, closely connected with Chiang Mai, requested Siamese protection and even sent tribute and one of her princes to Bangkok because Burma through Chiang Tung tried to exercise suzerainty over its territory. King Mongkut sent mostly Lān Nā troops who, however, failed to subdue Chiang Tung. In the end, Chiang Rung managed to stay independent of Burma but became part of China.[62]

In the decades after 1800, with return to peace, the decline of Burmese power and the advance of the British in Burma, Western and in particular British interest in mercantile connections with

---

62 Nearly one hundred years later, parts of territory formerly under Lān Nā or under her influence, but now under British Burma (M. Pan, Chiang Tung) and French Laos (west of the Mä Khōng, Saya Burī) briefly returned to Thailand when Thai troops occupied them between 1940 and 1947 in connection with the events of World War II.

Lān Nā revived. That interest was not limited to future trade with northernmost Siam alone but extended to trade with Yünnan by means of a railway from a Burmese harbor such as from Moulmein to Mä Sariang and Chiang Mai and on to Chiang Sän, Chiang Tung, Chiang Rung, and possibly further. Several surveys were made between 1837 and c. 1890 to select a route but in the end the project was abandoned.

Trade with northern Siam was conducted from Bangkok chiefly along the rivers. Western trade with Lān Nā picked up from about 1860, soon after the Bowring Treaty between Great Britain and Siam in 1855, when British firms began to buy concessions from local princes to cut the vast teak forests and to sell British-manufactured goods. They were soon followed by merchants of other nations. The first special treaty concerning northern Thailand was concluded in 1874 between Siam and the government of India in order to regulate commercial intercourse between Burma and the city-states or territories of Chiang Mai, Lamphūn, and Lampāng. A new treaty of 1883, abrogating the one of 1874, provided for the appointment of a British consul in Chiang Mai, who would thus become the first foreign diplomat in the North, and the setting up of an international court with Thai judges and the consul for cases involving British subjects. In 1884 British vice-consul F. B. Gould arrived.

While the first paper money, *mai* หมาย, was slowly introduced in Bangkok from 1853 on, the North preferred to hold on to its old money made from silver, or to use central Thai metal currency; but important commercial deals were usually made in British-issued Burmese rupees, *thäp* แถบ, which needed no exchange because they were acceptable among Thais and hilltribes from Burma to China, Laos, and Vietnam. Even ordinary British coins were accepted because of their known, reliable amount of silver.

With the British occupying Burma and the French advancing from the east, some traditional city-states lost part of their possessions under pressure from England and especially from France. Nān, for instance, lost its vassal Müang Sing to newly created French Laos. A border treaty between Britain and Siam in 1894, treaties between France and Siam in 1893 and 1904, and a treaty between Britain and France in 1896 resulted in Thailand's present borders with Burma and Laos.

The process of incorporating the semi-independent city-states of Lān Nā into the kingdom of Siam demanded a great many legal and administrative changes, both in Lān Nā and in Bangkok, and was further complicated by Bangkok's effort to overhaul at the same time the entire country's administration system and the legal codes, to introduce Western-style economic and social concepts, and to phase out the traditional slavery and debt-bondage system, in order to become a modern state, a partner acceptable to the great world powers of the time. The changes in Lān Nā have to be seen in the greater context of Siam as a whole. Most of them were gradually carried out in the reign of King Chulalongkorn (1868–1910).

Many of these changes were bitterly resented and even opposed, not only in Lān Nā. The time-honored bondman or serf system (in the West usually called a slave system though these slaves were generally well treated, in particular in Lān Nā) was an accepted social and religious institution. The slaves usually were debtors[63] who themselves or whose parents had defaulted on returning a greater amount of money, using their own person as collateral, and now stayed with the creditor until the debt was paid, either from their own work or by another person. They could change their creditor, or the creditor could exchange the slave for the money owed with another creditor. With the gradual abolishment of the system the creditor felt that now he had to pay wages to a person who actually owed him money. Also, for hundreds of years it had been a very meritorious act to forsake the service of one's bondman and to present him to a Buddha image in a monastery, so that he should serve the image. This great source of making merit was now closed. The final in a series of laws was promulgated in 1905 and not only "freed" all types of serfs but also ended the system of compulsory annual labor (corvée) for a prince or other superior which greatly affected their revenue.

Reform and standardization of the provincial administration was a dire necessity because in the course of time different systems had developed in various parts of Siam; administration had become complicated and often unmanageable. For example, the south of Siam was under the Klāhōm, a minister usually concerned with trade and some military matters; the Phra Khlang, usually in charge of finances, was also responsible for foreign affairs, trade, and oversaw the government of the towns on the coast along the

---

63 There were several categories of slaves, among them a sizeable percentage of "honorary slaves," viz. free persons including high-ranking government officials who voluntarily pledged to serve a Buddha statue or a stūpa.

northern end of the Gulf of Siam. In northern central Siam, under the Mahāt Thai, semi-hereditary governors ruled their provinces; and in Lān Nā, of course, the princes, in particular the king of Chiang Mai, were vassals and in most matters practically independent. But in the eyes of Western nations and for the growing local foreign community, the king of Siam alone became more and more the person ultimately responsible for what went on in all parts of the country. In the case of Lān Nā, in particular Chiang Mai, the execution of orders from Bangkok or the adherence to contracts was not always guaranteed. It was to be feared that the mishandling of forest leases or some other action would lead to British protests and worse.[64]

The beginnings of the reform of the interior administration can be dated to 1874 with the appointment in Bangkok of a Council of State, of a Privy Council. In the same year, Bangkok sent to Chiang Mai the first resident royal commissioner whose task it was to oversee local administration, to watch over contracts such as forest leases, to slowly limit the prerogatives of the local ruler, and to prepare the way to bring the northern city-states under control of the central administration as provinces that were no longer ruled by the local princes. At the same time, the princes' loss of political power had to be balanced in order not to damage too severely their sources of income.

---

64 Surely for cause, the above-mentioned treaties of 1874 and 1883 contained the clause "the said judges (at the Chiang Mai court) and the Prince of Chiengmai shall endeavour to prevent owners of forests from executing agreements with more than one party for the same timber or forests" (le May, op.cit. p.55).

But reform really came only in 1892 with the appointment of a European-style cabinet of twelve ministries with the king acting like a prime minister though he still was an absolute monarch with no constitution to follow. Provincial administration was now placed with the newly created Ministry of Interior. Prince Damrong Rajanubhab (1862–1943) headed the ministry from that year until 1915, during the crucial first period.

The prince devised a pyramid-like administration and taxation system, the base of which was upcountry and the peak of which was Bangkok, using features of previous local government. At the base was the *mū bān* (village); several villages formed a *tambon* (county, precinct, community). The leaders of village and county were locally chosen. Several *tambon* formed an *amphö* (district), several *amphö* formed a *jangwat* (province), and several *jangwat* formed a *monthon* (circle). The heads of the last three were ultimately nominated from Bangkok and initially nearly always were people from Bangkok though locals were encouraged to send their children to Bangkok for proper education so that they might return as government administrators.

The first *monthon* were established in Khōrāt (1893) and Ayuthayā (1894). Gradually, other *monthon* were added until the *monthon* system extended over the whole country. The head of a *monthon* was a royal resident commissioner, the *thesā phi-bān* เทศาภิบาล, later called *samuha thesā phibān* สมุหเทศาภิบาล, or *thesā* for short, with power similar to the commissionership previously established in Chiang Mai, in particular to override local grandees, to organize revenue collection, and to issue law-like orders. At the head of a province was the *jao müang* เจ้าเมือง or governor.

Lān Nā was divided into two *monthon*: Mahā Rāt and Phāyap. Monthon Mahā Rāt consisted of the provinces Nān, Phrä, and Lampāng; Phāyap comprised Chiang Mai, Lamphūn, Chiang Rāi, and Mä Hòng Sòn. The provinces went directly back to the former city-states with the exception of Mä Hòng Sòn, a new settlement established only in 1831 at first as a centre for hunting and training elephants. The *monthon* were abolished after the change of government from absolute to constitutional monarchy in 1932, and the provinces came directly under the Ministry of Interior; the title of the governor changed from *jao müang* to the present title, *phū wā rāchakān* ผู้ว่าราชการ. In 1972, the southern part of the vast province of Chiang Rāi became a province of its own, Phayao.

It speaks for the benevolent firmness of the Siamese kings, for the diplomatic and human tact on the part of the Siamese royal commissioners, and for the perception of the local princes, that the Bangkok-induced political demise of Lān Nā's kings and nobles did not lead to serious rebellion. King Inthanon of Chiang Mai even gave his daughter, Dārā Rasmī, in marriage to King Chulalongkorn. Elsewhere resistance to reform was stronger, usually caused by loss of revenue because income now was inspected by and shared in the form of taxes with Bangkok. In 1902, the *rājā* of Pattani had to be arrested and was exiled to Phitsanulōk. As for Lān Nā, in 1889 there began a strong local protest against certain farmed-out tax monopolies which, under the leadership of a certain Phayā Prāp Songkhrām, turned into a short-lived political opposition and revolt against Bangkok influence. In 1902, there was also an uprising in Phrä, carried out by Shan immigrants who were helped by local nobles and their wealthy friends who chiefly resented the reduction of their income.

The administrative integration of the former city-states also had to be accompanied by physical incorporation beginning with improved communication systems. Travel by boat and on "roads" to Bangkok was exhausting and slow. At high water level and with a good crew, the 870-km boat journey down to Bangkok could be made within ten days; usually it took about three weeks. But the journey upriver took one and a half to two months because of the many rapids (now covered by the water of the Bhumibol Reservoir), and once, in 1867, the missionary Dr. McGilvary needed three months. Because of the slow connection, mail from Europe and even from North America was sent to Chiang Mai via Moulmein in Burma; the two towns had, since 1884, a regular mail service every two weeks. The Siamese Post began its service in 1883 and introduced a first set of stamps of five values; but for many more years private contractors transported the mail between Bangkok and the North.

Speed and quality of communication with Bangkok increased dramatically when the first telegraph line to Chiang Mai was opened in 1888; by 1905, one could even telephone (sometimes) from Chiang Mai to Chiang Rāi.

The northern railway line reached Phitsanulōk in 1907, Den Chai (Phrä's station) in 1909, Lampāng in 1916 and Chiang Mai in 1919 (at present, 751 km). The Northern Line, as it was called, was officially opened to the public on 1 January 1922. Whereas in 1913 the railway plus road trip to Chiang Mai took eleven days, now the twice-weekly express took only thirteen and a half hours.[65] Financially, the northern line then was no loss either; it produced 6 percent earnings on the invested capital, not counting interest on loans.

Private cars, motor buses, and lorries began arriving in Chiang Mai probably around 1910 or 1915; by 1925, Chiang Mai was said to have about 170 motor vehicles, all brought up by train, sometimes as separate parts. The first car to be driven all the way from Bangkok to Chiang Mai, except across rivers, arrived here only in around 1930–1932. Thailand's road-building program began only under Prime Minister Phibun Songkhrām (1938–1944, 1948–1957). The last stretch of the road from Bangkok to Chiang Mai (c. 700 km) received an all-weather surface in 1972.

More or less regular flights between Bangkok and Chiang Mai are said to have been operated in the late 1930s but scheduled passenger service began in the 1950s. In the 1960s, travel by air (counting from one's departure at home in Chiang Mai to arrival at one's destination in Bangkok) took about three hours, of which roughly two hours were spent in the air. Today, because of traffic jams at either end, time-consuming check-in requirements and slow baggage retrieval, it takes the same time and more, with an actual flying time of about fifty-five minutes.

As has been mentioned, from about 1875 on, the arrangement of having northern vassal kings or vassal princes actually rule

---

65 For comparison: in 1993, according to the time-table, the daily Express took 13 hours and 25 minutes, the daily Special Express took 12 hours and 25 minutes, and the daily four-coach diesel-electric railcar Sprinter (introduced in 1991) took 10 hours and 50 minutes. In 1998 the Sprinter had slowed down and needed 12 hours and 40 minutes.

their territory was slowly discontinued. The first governor from Bangkok arrived in Chiang Mai in 1874, still more in a capacity as councillor than as director of affairs. His successors from 1877 on had increased powers. The last prince of Chiang Mai, Jao Käo Nowarat, had only token power and largely a representative function. After his death in 1939, no further Chiang Mai ruler was appointed from Bangkok and thus ended officially the role of the vassal king. But the king of Thailand and the royal Thai court protocol still acknowledge the northern princes, *jao nāi fāi nüa* เจ้านายฝ่ายเหนือ, and thus honor and remember those northern kings and princes of old who were pivotal in the creation of modern Thailand.

The so-called hill tribes, Mong (Mäo, Miao), Akha, Lisu, Yao Musö, etc., are recent immigrants who have been arriving from Laos and Burma only since about 1880. The latest newcomers are Palaung, who since 1983 have been settling in the area of Dòi Āng Khāng ดอยอ่างขาง west of Fāng; their original home was in north Burma. The Karen, however, are a possible exception; they may have lived in Lān Nā's western hills for centuries.

APPENDIX I

Lān Nā Rulers of the Mang Rāi Dynasty
1263–1578

The Court in Chiang Rāi - Chiang Mai - Chiang Sän

According to the Chronicle of Chiang Mai (CMA) and the chronicle Jinakālamālī (JKM)[1]

1. Mang Rāi[2]	1263–1281	Chiang Rāi	(CMA)
	1286–1296	Wiang Kum Kām	(CMA)
	1296–1317	Chiang Mai	(CMA)
	1263–1292	Chiang Rāi	(JKM)
	1296–1311	Chiang Mai	(JKM)

---

1 Due to a different beginning of the Yuan and Western calendar year, some of the dates below may fall in the first months of the succeeding year.

2 According to CMA, Mang Rāi first founded Chiang Rāi and lived there, then moved to Wiang Kum Kām, probably a rebuilt former Mon settlement near Chiang Mai, and then founded Chiang Mai and moved there.

2. Chai Songkhrām[3]	1318	Chiang Mai	(CMA)
	1318–1327	Chiang Rāi	(CMA)
	1311	Chiang Mai	(JKM)
	1311–1325	Chiang Rāi	(JKM)
3. Sän Phū[4]	1327	Chiang Rāi	(CMA)
	1327–1338	Chiang Sän	(CMA)
	1325–1327	Chiang Rāi	(JKM)
	1327–1334	Chiang Sän	(JKM)
4. Kham Fū	1338–1345	Chiang Sän	(CMA)
	1334–1336	Chiang Sän	(JKM)
5. Phā Yū[5]	1345–1367	Chiang Mai	(CMA)
	1337–1339	Chiang Sän	(JKM)
	1339–1355	Chiang Mai	(JKM)
6. Kü Nā	1367–1388	(CMA)	
	1355–1385	(JKM)	

---

3 According to CMA, he stayed only four months in Chiang Mai, invested his son Sän Phū as local vassal, and moved to Chiang Rāi.

4 According to CMA, he founded Chiang Sän and lived there. CMA says that there are two chronicles with different dates for the founding of Chiang Sän: 1327 and early 1329.

5 He moved the court back to Chiang Mai, according to JKM, after two years in Chiang Sän; but according to CMA, he simply stayed on in Chiang Mai where he had been ruling as vassal of his father, Kham Fū.

7. Sän Müang Mä[6]	1400–1401	(CMA)
	1385–1401	(JKM)
8. Säm Fang Kän[7] (Mä Nai)	1401–1442	(CMA)
	1401–1441	(JKM)
9. Tilok(a Rät)	1442–1487	(CMA)
	1441–1487	(JKM)
10. Yòt Chiang Rāi	1487–1495	(CMA, JKM)
11. (Phra Müang) Käo	1495–1526	(CMA, JKM)
12. Ket (1st time)	1526–1538	(CMA, JKM)[8]
13. Thāo Chai	1538–1543	
14. Ket (2nd time)	1543–1545	
15. Mahā Thewī Jīrap(r)aphā	1545–1546	
16. Upay(a)o	1546–1547	
Vacant	1547–1551	
17. Mä Ku	1551–1564	
18. Wisuttha Thewī	1564–1578	

---

6 CMA also says that Sän Müang Mä ruled for twenty-five years.

7 According to a contemporary stone inscription, he was enthroned in 1402.

8 JKM ends with the year 1527.

APPENDIX II

Jao Jet Ton: "The Seven Princes"

The Thip Chāng ทิพย์ช้าง or Thip Jak ทิพย์จักก์ dynasty, was a dynasty of princes ruling over central and western Lān Nā during the eighteenth to twentieth centuries. There were three main lines, viz. Lampāng, Chiang Mai, and Lamphūn. The beginnings of the dynasty go back to before 1775, i.e. to before the period during which the Burmese were expelled from Lān Nā (1775–1804). The seven princes, or Jao Jet Ton เจ้าเจ็ดตน, were brothers who belonged to that dynasty. Together with their descendants, they were instrumental in the expulsion of the Burmese and then in the administration and rebuilding of central and western Lān Nā (Chiang Mai, Lamphūn, Lampāng, Chiang Rāi, Phayao, Tāk, Mä Hòng Sòn). That is why sometimes the dynasty is also called the "Dynasty of the Seven Princes" สายสกุลเจ้าเจ็ดตน even though they were not the founders but the third generation.

The dynasty took its origin in very troubled times. As has been recounted above, Lān Nā, i.e. approximately northern Thailand, had formerly been an independent kingdom with vassals in Burma and Laos. More technically speaking, it had been a powerful conglomerate of city-states under the suzerainty of the renowned city-state Chiang Mai. During a period of what probably was a self-induced decay caused by overspending, among other things, Lān Nā had been annexed by Burma in 1558 as a Burmese sub-kingdom, nominally still headed by Thai Yuan princes ruling over now fractured principalities, but in fact controlled by Burmese residents, governors, or military commanders (*myowun, myoza, sitke*) with locally garrisoned Burmese soldiers at their disposition.

The Thai Yuan population of Lān Nā (formerly wrongly called "Lāo" in Bangkok) had frequently rebelled against the Burmese without being able to regain independence; the Burmese could always call in vast numbers of soldiers, and the Yuan themselves did not present a united front to oppose the Burmese.

Burma-occupied Lān Nā had also been attacked and raided by armies from Laos and Ayuthayā (Siam, central Thailand), and since some of the Burmese officials were easygoing and others oppressive, the Yuan leaders had sometimes sided with the Burmese against the new aggressors, and sometimes with the foreign aggressors against the Burmese occupation forces in Lān Nā, hoping to achieve independence.

Many of Lān Nā's city-states and villages had also been fighting under their own war lords against each other or against the Burmese occupation forces or against Yuan or Burmese individuals, always ready to change sides for an immediate, short-term profit.

This had caused a latent, many-sided civil war in Lān Nā which in turn had caused the Burmese, between 1701 and 1733, to divide Lān Nā into two parts in order to better control the area: East Lān Nā with the capital Chiang Sän, and West Lān Na with the capital Chiang Mai. Lampāng belonged to East Lān Nā, Lamphūn to West Lān Nā.

In the years around 1730 Lampāng had neither a ruling prince nor a governor, only four city elders, *phò müang* พ่อเมือง, and was subject to raids from its neighbors, mostly Lamphūn. A few officials could do little in administrating and defending the country. The respected abbot of Wat Chumphū วัดชุมพู asked Nāi Thip Jak (or Thip Chāng), a hunter born in about 1690,[1] to dislodge Thāo Mahā Yot วัดเจ็ดยอด of Lamphūn and his marauding band from Wat Phra Thāt Lampāng Luang, south of Lampāng, where they had made their camp. Nāi Thip Jak was an intelligent and brave commoner, good at shooting with gun and bow สีนาดและธนู. He accepted on condition that he would be given three hundred armed men and, in case of success, that he would become king of Lampāng.

In the dark, Thip Jak and three trusted men crept through a water conduit into the monastery compound, shot Thāo Mahā Yot dead, and then with their group put the Lamphūn band to flight.

Thereupon in 1732/33 Thip Jak was made king of Lampāng by general popular choice with the name / title Phrayā Sulawa Rüchai, Lord of Müang Nakhòn Lampāng พระยาสุลวะฤๅชัย เจ้าเมืองนคอร (ลำปาง).[2] He probably was a little over forty years old.

---

1 Assuming he died in 1760 at age seventy.

2 The spelling of the title is not uniform. Variants include, for instance, สุลัวลือไชย and สุละวะลือไชย.

The Burmese did not interfere. The Lampāng country became peaceful again.

Later he asked the Burmese to confirm his title, and the Burmese king, his overlord, invested him in c. 1735 as Lampāng ruler with the title Phrayā Chai Songkhrām พระยาชัยสงคราม. Occasionally his two titles get mixed or are compounded into one and he is called, somewhat incorrectly, Phrayā Sulawa Rüchai Songkhrām.

The rest of his reign was rather peaceful, except for yet another raiding party from Lamphūn that also tried to assassinate him in his own house, and he died in 1759/60 after a reign of twenty-seven years.

He and his queen, Nāng Phimphā พิมพา or Phimalā พิมาลา, were the founders of the dynasty. Some say they had eight children, four boys and four girls, but the Chiang Mai chronicle ตำนานพื้นเมืองเชียงใหม่ says they had only six, four boys and two girls.

After his death the dignitaries and people proclaimed Jao Chāi Kāo เจ้าชายแก้ว as king of Lampāng, a son of the deceased Phrayā Chai Songkhrām. He again was chosen by general consent, likely in about 1760. He was born perhaps in about 1722 and now was probably not quite forty years old.[3]

Soon a general civil war broke out in the Lampāng, Lamphūn, and southern Chiang Mai regions, local warlords raiding one another. One reason seems to have been that Chai Kāo's succession was opposed. Chāi Kāo and his brother Phò Rüan fled to Phrä, returned with a group of men from Phrä but were unable

---

3 Assuming he was twenty when his first child, Kāwila, was born in 1842.

to overcome their opposition in Lampāng. Phò Rüan was killed in an encounter, and Chāi Käo had to return to Phrä.

Since all of western and central Lān Nā was now in chaos, the Burmese came with a strong army and took Chiang Mai in 1763. The Burmese chief commander, Apyakāmanī อะพยะกามะนี,[4] stayed on in Chiang Mai and sent troops all over Lān Nā to restore order. The cities of Lampāng and Phrä even welcomed the Burmese, who did no ill.

They met Chāi Käo in Phrä, but the Burmese generals were unable to decide who was in the right, Chāi Käo or his adversaries, and so they sent him to the king of Burma to decide. The king ordered Chāi Käo to be restored to his Lampāng rule and invested him in 1764 with the somewhat Shan-sounding title Jao Fā ("lord of heaven," i.e. ruling prince) Singharāchathānī, Jao Fā Luang Chāi Käo เจ้าฟ้าสิงหราชธานี เจ้าฟ้าหลวงชายแก้ว. He returned to Lampāng and his chief opponents became his ministers, Thāo Lin Kān ท้าวลิ้นก่าน and Sän Phün แสนพื้น.

After some time, Chāi Käo and his old enemies quarreled again. The Burmese generals now authorized a water ordeal to solve the simmering conflict once and for all, a contest between Chāi Käo and Thāo Lin Kān of who could stay longer under water. The loser would be executed. Chāi Käo won, some of his opponents were caught and killed, and others escaped. These again became very troublesome until a Burmese commander finally ordered them to be caught and killed, which was done.

---

4 He is also called Pō "general" Aphaikhāmanī โป๊อภัยคามินี, in Western literature often spelled Abhayagāmani.

Here it should be mentioned that Chāi Kāo and his queen, Nāng Janthā Thewī นางจันทาเทวี, had altogether ten children, seven boys, and three girls. According to the Chiang Mai Chronicle, they were born in two-year intervals between 1742 and 1760/61. The eldest was Jao Kāwila (or Nāi Kāwila, as the central Thais called him), born on 31 October 1742 at about 6 p.m. He is considered the ancestor of the Chiang Mai line of the dynasty, or the "na Chiang Mai" ณ เชียงใหม่ family. The seven boys, who were close to each other, were collectively called "the seven princes," or Jao Jet Ton:

1. Jao Khanān[5] Kāwila   เจ้าขนานกาวิละ   b. 1742
2. Jao Kham Som   เจ้าคำสม   b. 1744/45
3. Jao Nòi Thamma Langkā   เจ้าน้อยธรรมลังกา   b. 1746/47
4. Jao Duang Thip   เจ้าดวงทิพย์   b. 1748/49
5. Jao Mū Lā   เจ้าหมูหล้า   b. 1754/55
6. Jao Kham Fan   เจ้าคำฝั้น   b. 1756/57
7. Jao Bun Mā   เจ้าบุญมา   b. 1760/61

Some time after Chai Kāo's enemies had been removed, most of the Burmese military left for Ayuthayā to reinforce the armies which were to seize Ayuthayā on 7 April 1767. Lampāng also sent a force under Jao Kham Som, the second of the seven princes, then a young man of about twenty-two.

The remaining Burmese, now without proper supervision, promptly began to tyrannize the people. King Chāi Kāo went to Chiang Mai to inform Apyakāmani, the Burmese chief com-

---

5 Jao = Prince, lord; khanān (or nān หนาน) = ex-monk; nòi = ex-novice.

mander, and to work with him. The year 1765 began badly. On 30 January there was a heavy earthquake; people who were standing fell down. On 20 February there was a solar eclipse. Later in the year, the ruler of Lamphūn and some of his people revolted against Apyakāmani. This again brought about a war in all of western Lān Nā. Apyakāmani had to withdraw to Burma and Chāi Kǎo of Lampāng went with him.

The victorious Lamphūn group now on their part began to oppress the people in Lampāng, extorting "cowries and silver" as the Chiang Mai Chronicle puts it. Kāwila as leader and his brothers managed the administration as well as possible, trying to steer a middle course and avoiding the worst. They obviously did not have the means to resist the Lamphūn foes openly.

Soon Apyakāmani returned from Burma with an army under General Asāwon อแสหว่ร[6] to restore order in Lān Nā. With them came Chāi Kǎo. They seized Lamphūn and Chiang Mai.

Apyakāmani had now been appointed myowun โมยหวาน or "resident" of Chiang Mai and stayed on as the chief commander but he could not really restore Burmese supremacy because there were insurrections and raids in several places, with Yuan, Shan, and Burmese all mixed together in them. Kāwila as commander went and successfully suppressed the major raiding band under the *sitke* of Thön, a Yuan, who was set to raid Lampāng.

Apyakāmani died in 1768/69. Many Yuan seem to have been content with him, and it was probably also due to his humane

---

6 Also called Asäwunkī อแซวุ่นกี้.

ways that Burma then could still hold on to Chiang Mai and
Lān Nā.[7]

He was replaced in the same year by Mäng Ne Myōkāmanī
แมง เหน่ โมยกามะนี, called by the Yuan, Pō Hua Khāo, โป่หัวขาว, i.e.
"General Whitehead," because he used to wear a white cloth
around his head. He too was harassed by insurgencies and revolts.
His character was gruff and he was also disliked by the Burmese.

It is probably too much to claim that his actions were the reason
why Burma finally lost Lān Lā but the fact is that Lān Nā's most
serious and finally successful rebellion under Jā Bān and Kāwila
began in his time. He had a way to incense people. Soon after
his arrival, a Yuan who was serving as local Burmese commander,
Sitke Nòi Phrom, with a group of followers openly challenged
him in Chiang Mai town and a short fight left many dead.

In 1770 (or 1764), the Burmese army, supplemented by a
detachment from Lampāng (under princes Kāwila and Duang
Thip, adds one source), went to wage war in Lān Chāng, viz. in
Luang Phra Bāng territory (or in Wiang Jan, i.e. Vientiane) in
Laos. The background and outcome of that war (or these wars)
did not interest the authors of our sources very much, so they
said nothing about them. But they were sufficiently impressed
by one item, which they did record, viz. that the Burmese troops
here obtained, and subsequently presented to their king, a *nāng
sām phiu* นางสามผิว, a "three-skin lady," which means, in Yuan

---

7 Another high Burmese official well-liked by his people, Yuan and Burmese alike, was the myowun or resident of Chiang Sän, Mang Bara Saphäk,
who died in 1740/41.

tradition, a woman whose skin is pale in the morning, then pink around noon, and rosy in the evening.

It is also said that in this time, around 1770, a Burmese order was issued (by whom and where is not recorded) that in all upcountry states (and this would include Lān Nā) the men had totattoo their legs black, and the women had to pierce their ears and insert a rolled piece of palm leaf, Burmese fashion.

Local fights between remaining oppressive Burmese troops and the Yuan continued. A notable event was when one of the Yuan officials, the Phrayā Jā Bān named Bun Mā พระยาจ่าบ้าน บุญมา, revolted against General Whitehead in Chiang Mai. Bun Mā's brother, Nāi Mòng นายหม่อง was killed, and Bun Mā had to retreat.

Our Thai sources do not seem to record the reason for Jā Ban's quarrel with General Whitehead, but the Burmese Glass Palace Chronicle does. At the core possibly was a question of protocol and injured pride. As the chronicle explains, Jā Bān had received an order from the Burmese king regarding the administrative relationship between himself and the Burmese governor. Instead of giving this order himself to the governor, he sent his younger brother. The *myowun* insisted that Jā Bān come himself. Jā Bān refused, so the governor sent people to fetch him. This then resulted in the armed confrontation.

Thereupon Jā Bān went with his group to Lampāng, met with Jao Kāwila and his brothers, and concluded here the agreement with them that was the beginning of the end of the Burmese in Lān Nā and which, ultimately, would create present northern Thailand. As the Chiang Mai Chronicle puts it: "(Phrayā Jā Bān led his group to Lampāng and) concluded a solemn agreement with Jao Kāwila, the eldest son of Jao Fā Luang Chai Käo; and the seven brother princes swore to each other to be firmly united."[8] Even if the chronicle does not say exactly what that agreement was about, it is clear from the outcome that they wanted to push the Burmese out with the help of the Siamese at the next opportunity, and that they would act together according to one plan, not piece-meal.

Jā Bān then went to the Burmese commander who was with his troops in Laos, to complain about General Whitehead.

In the meantime the Siamese, whose capital Ayuthayā had been destroyed in 1767, had regrouped under a new king, Tāksin, and had set up a new capital further downstream, in the hamlet Thon Burī opposite another hamlet, Bāng Kok (present Bangkok). For an unknown reason they came up with an army and besieged Chiang Mai between 18 and 26 March 1771, but they could not seize the city and returned home.

The Burmese general and the Jā Bān Bun Mā now came back from Laos to Chiang Mai.

The next events probably happened in 1773–1774.

The Burmese commanders in Chiang Mai intended to attack the new Siamese capital Thon Burī and began preparing troops and boats. Here was the opportunity to destroy Burmese power in Lān Nā for which Jā Bān and Kāwila with his brothers had been waiting.

---

8 The wording in the Chiang Mai Chronicle is: "(พระยาจ่าบ้านพาหมู่ไปถึง นครลำปาง) ปฏิจจปราสรัยกับเจ้ากาวิละ ตนเป็นลูกอ้ายฟ้าหลวงชายแก้ว แลเจ้า 7 องค์ พี่น้อง ตั้งสัจจะต่อกันเป็นอันมั่นอันแกน".

Ja Bān sent word to Kāwila in Lampāng: They would now begin with their revolt against the Burmese. Kāwila was to make preparations in Lampāng while he, Ja Bān, would go down and bring up the Siamese army.

Ja Bān now told the Burmese commanders he would volunteer and go ahead to clear the Mä Ping rapids[9] of driftwood in order to facilitate the descent of the main army. He received seventy Burmese and Shan, and fifty Yuan, and at Hòt, above the first rapids, the Yuan killed and dispersed the Burmese and Shan.

Then he went as quickly as possible downriver to meet King Tāksin and his generals and invited them up to fight the Burmese. Preparations were made in great haste. The army was divided in two parts. One under Ja Bān went upriver and encamped at Thā Wang Tān ท่าวังตาล south of Chiang Mai. The other, under generals Surasī and Jakrī (founder of the present Chakrī dynasty) went via Lampāng. Ja Bān, who arrived first, was beaten by the Burmese, but when the Siamese army arrived with the Lampāng contingent under Princes Kāwila, Kham Som, and the other brothers, the Burmese could not hold their position and withdrew from Chiang Mai. The joint Siamese-Yuan armies seized Chiang Mai during the night from Saturday to Sunday, 14–15 January 1775.

For Kāwila and his brothers, the situation held a personal drama. Vigilant General Whitehead had, some time before, summoned King Chai Käo of Lampāng to come and stay in Chiang

---

9 Before the present Yan Hī dam was built resulting in the Bhumibol Reservoir, the Ping had here over thirty rapids, some particularly dangerous for shipping.

Mai supposedly in order to assist from here with the country's administration while Kāwila and his brothers administrated Lampāng locally. When the hostilities began, King Chai Käo was imprisoned by the Burmese in Chiang Mai while Kāwila and his allies went about to seize the town from them. After the departure of the Burmese, it was found that he was still alive in prison. The Burmese had spared his life.

This first successful joint military operation was the beginning of the later complete merger of Lān Nā with Siam that created what is now north Thailand. Right from the outset it was clear that the north was a vassal that accepted the overlordship of the south. King Tāksin's first official acts concerning his new vassal, western Lān Nā, were the nominations necessary for the administration of the three liberated cities.

For Chiang Mai, he appointed:
- Phrayā Jā Bān, to be Phrayā Chiang Mai (ruler, ruling prince, king);
- Nāi Nòi Kòn Käo นายน้อยก้อนแก้ว, grandson or nephew, หลาน, of Phrayā Jā Bān, to be the Uparāt อุปราช (deputy ruler).

For Lamphūn, he appointed:
- Sitke Khäng เช็กคายแดง, to be Phrayā Lamphūn.
- Nāi Nòi Ton Tò นายน้อยตอนต้อ, younger brother of the latter, to be the Uparāt.
- Nāi Nòi Phōthi Dòn Thòng นายน้อยโพธิดอนทอง, to be Phrayā Suriwong สุริวงศ์.

King Tāksin returned south via Phra Thāt Lampāng Luang พระ
ธาตุลำปางหลวง down to central Thailand. In Lampāng, he made
the following nominations:

- Jao Kāwila, to be Phrayā Nakhòn (Lampāng); presumably
  his father, King Chai Käo, retired from the administration.
- Jao Thamma Langkā เจ้าธรรมลังกา, to be the Uparāt.[10]

Romance was not absent. King Tāksin's general, Jao Phrayā Süa
เสือ alias Jao Phrayā Surasī สุรสีห์, fell in love with Nāng Sī Anōcha
นางศรีอโนชา, a sister of the seven brothers (b. 1750), married her,[11]
and then followed.

This was the beginning of a long and fruitful cooperation between the Jao Jet Ton and their descendants, and their overlords,
the kings of Siam, later Thailand. It was chiefly due to Jā Bān
and Kāwila and his brothers that Lān Nā took the initiative and
willingly united with Siam for mutual benefit. Later generations
of the Dynasty of the Seven Princes continued this policy.

The last Jao Luang เจ้าหลวง "Great Lord," as the northern rulers
were later commonly known, was Jao Käo Nowarat เจ้าแก้วนวรัฐฯ. By
then, times had changed, the rulers no longer "ruled" and were
no longer real "vassals"; their role was largely representative and
honorific. Born in 1862, he became acting ruler in 1909/10 and
was invested by King Vajiravudh in 1911. He died in 1939. After
him, no more nominations were made.

---

10 One source says that Jao Kham Som was made Uparāt in Lampāng,
and Jao Thamma Langkā was made Phrayā Rāchawong, which is not unlikely,
because Kham Som was the elder.

11 One source specifies her status: "ได้เป็นห้ามกรมพระราชวังมหาสุรสีห์".

The Beginnings of the Thip Jak Dynasty
and
Major Positions of the Seven Princes

Name	Born / died	Year of Accession	
Thip Jak / Thip Chāng	?– 1757	c. 1732	King of Lampāng
Chai Kăo	?–?	c. 1757	King of Lampāng
1. Jao Kāwila	1742–1816	1775	King of Lampāng
		1782	King of Chiang Mai
2. Jao Kham Som	1744–1794/95	1782 or 1786/87	King of Lampāng
3. Jao Thamma Langkā	1746–1821	1816	King of Chiang Mai
4. Jao Duang Thip	1748–1825	1794/95	King of Lampāng
5. Jao Mū Lā	1754–1815/16	1794/95	Uparāt, Lampāng
6. Jao Kham Fan	1756–1825	1814	King of Lamphūn
		1821	King of Chiang Mai
7. Jao Bun Mā	1760–1826/27	1815/16	King of Lamphūn

APPENDIX III

Vassal Rulers of Chiang Mai
1775–1939

Note: act. = acting; inv. = royal investiture

1775 inv.–c. 1781	Phrayā Wichian Prākān พระยาวิเชียรปราการ
	(Bun Mā บุญมา, Phrayā Jā Bān พระยาจ่าบ้าน)
1782 inv.–1816	Kāwila พระเจ้ากาวิละ
1816 inv.–1821	Thammalangkā เจ้าหลวงธัมมลังกา
	(Jao Chāng Phüak เจ้าช้างเผือก)
1821 act.	Kham Fan เจ้าหลวงคำฝั้น
1823 inv.–1825	(Mahā Suphathra Rācha มหาสุภัทรราชะ;
	Jao Sethī เจ้าเศรษฐี)
1825 act.	Phutthawong เจ้าหลวงพุทธวงศ์
1826/27 inv.–1846	(Jao Kākawannāthibodī (เจ้า)กากวรรณาทิปราช)
1846/47 act.	Mahōtra Prathet พระเจ้ามโหตรประเทศ
1847/48 inv.–1855	(Khanān Mahāwong ขนานมหาวงศ์)
1856 inv.–1870	Kāwilōrot พระเจ้ากาวิโลรส
	(Khanān Suriyawong ขนานสุริยวงศ์;
	Jao Chīwit Āo เจ้าชีวิตอ้าว)
1870 act.	Inthawichayānon พระเจ้าอินทวิชยานนท์

1873 inv.–1897	(Jao Inthanon เจ้าอินทนนท์,
	Jao Luang Tā Khāo เจ้าหลวงตาขาว)
1897 act.	Inthawarōrot Suriyawong เจ้าอินทวโรรสสุริยวงศ์
1901 inv.–1910	(Jao Nòi Suriya เจ้าน้อยสุริยะฯ)
1910 act.	Kāo Nowarat พลตรี เจ้าแก้วนวรัฐฯ
1911 inv.–1939	(Jao Kāo เจ้าแก้วฯ)

Selected Bibliography

Historical Texts

The History of Queen Jām Thewī of Lamphūn
"Histoire de Nang Kiam Tévī." In Auguste Pavie, *Etudes diverses* (2), Paris, 1898, p. 145–166.

Camille Notton. *Annales du Siam*, 2e volume, Chronique de La:p'un—Histoire de la dynastie Chamt'évi. Paris, 1930.

The Chronicle Cāmadevīvaṃsa, c. 1410

พระยาปริยัติธรรมธาดา (แพ ตาลลักษมณ์) / พระยาญาณวิจิตร์ (สิทธิ โลจนานนท์) "เรื่องจามเทวีวงศ์ พงศาสดารเมืองหริภุญชัย" กรุงเทพฯ หอพระสมุดวชิรญาณ 2463 (²2510).

Donald K. Swearer and Sommai Premchit. *The Legend of Queen Cāma. Bodhiraṃsi's Cāmadevīvaṃsa, a Translation and Commentary*. New York: State University of New York Press, 1998.

The Chronicle Mūlasāsanā, c. 1425–1510

สุด ศรีสมวงศ์ / พรหม ขมาลา "ตำนานมูลศาสนา" กรุงเทพฯ กรมศิลปากร 2482 (²2513).
ประเสริฐ ณ นคร "ตำนานมูลศาสนา" กรุงเทพฯ 2518.

The Chronicle Jinakālamālī, 1517–1527

แสง มนวิทูร "ชินกาลมาลีปกรณ์" กรุงเทพฯ กรมศิลปากร 2501 (²2510)

G. Coedès. "Jinakālamālinī. In G. Coedès, Documents sur l'histoire politique et religieuse du Laos occidental." *Bulletin de l'Ecole Française d'Extrême-Orient*, vol. 25, 1925: texte p. 36–72, traduction p. 73–140.

N. A. Jayawickrama. *The Sheaf of Garlands of the Epochs of the Conqueror. Being a Translation of Jinakālamālipakaranaṃ of Ratanapañña Thera of Thailand*. London: The Pali Text Society, 1968.

Hans Penth. *Jinakālamālī Index. An annotated Index to the Thailand Part of Ratanapañña's Chronicle Jinakālamālī*. Oxford: The Pali Text Society / Chiang Mai: Silkworm Books, 1994.

The Chiang Mai Chronicle, c. 1805–1827

อุดม รุ่งเรืองศรี "ตำนานพื้นเมืองเชียงใหม่ ฉบับ 700 ปี" เชียงใหม่ ศูนย์วัฒนธรรมจังหวัดเชียงใหม่ สถาบันราชภัฏเชียงใหม่ 2539.

Camille Notton (tr.). *Annales du Siam*, 3e volume: Chronique de Xieng Mai. Paris, 1932.
David K. Wyatt / Aroonrut Wichienkeeo (trs.). *The Chiang Mai Chronicle*. Chiang Mai: Silkworm Books, 1995 ([2]1998).

The Nān Chronicle, c. 1895

แสนหลวง ราชสมภาร "เรื่องราชวงศปกรณ" ใน "ประชุมพงศาวดาร" (10) กรุงเทพฯ 2462. Reprint: กรุงเทพฯ สำนักพิมพ์ก้าวหน้า 2507.
David K. Wyatt (tr. and ed.). *The Nan Chronicle*. Ithaca, New York: Cornell University, 1994.

Inscriptions

คณะกรรมการจัดพิมพ์เอกสารทางประวัติศาสตร์ . . . (บรรณาธิการ) "ประชุมศิลาจารึก" กรุงเทพฯ สำนักนายกรัฐมนตรี 2508 (ภาคที่ 3), 2513 (ภาคที่ 4)
ฮันส์ เพนธ์ (บรรณาธิการ) "คำจารึกที่ฐานพระพุทธรูปในนครเชียงใหม่" กรุงเทพฯ สำนักนายก รัฐมนตรี 2519.
กรรณิการ์ วิมลเกษม ฯลฯ (บรรณาธิการ) "จารึกล้านนา", ภาค 1 เล่ม 1 จารึกจังหวัดเชียงราย น่าน พะเยา แพร่, เล่ม 2 ภาพ, กรุงเทพฯ 2534.
ฮันส์ เพนธ์ / พรรณเพ็ญ เครือไทย / ศรีเลา เกษพรหม (บรรณาธิการ) "ประชุมจารึกล้านนา" สถาบันวิจัยสังคม มหาวิทยาลัยเชียงใหม่ 2540-2546 เล่ม 1-6.

Historical Legends

สงวน โชติสุขรัตน์ "ประชุมตำนานล้านนาไทย" กรุงเทพฯ สำนักพิมพ์โอเดียนสโตร์ พ.ศ. 2515 (2 เล่ม).
มานิต วัลลิโภดม "ตำนานสิงหนวัติกุมาร" คณะกรรมการจัดพิมพ์เอกสารทางประวัติศาสตร์ กรุงเทพฯ คณะกรรมการจัดพิมพ์เอกสารทางประวัติศาสตร์ สำนักนายกรัฐมนตรี 2516.
Camille Notton. *Annales du Siam*, 1er volume, Chroniques de Suvaṇṇa Khamdëng, Mahāthera Fā Bot, Suvaṇṇa K'ôm Kham, Siṅhanavati. Paris, 1926.

Historical Poetry

Lilit Yuan Phāi, c. 1475?
"ลิลิตยวนพ่าย" ฉบับหอสมุดแห่งชาติ กรุงเทพฯ สำนักพิมพ์คลังวิทยา 2512.
A. B. Griswold / Prasert na Nagara (trs., eds). "A Fifteenth-Century Historical Poem." (Lilit Yuan Phāi). In Cowan/Wolters (eds), *Southeast Asian History and Historiography*. Essays presented to D. G. E. Hall. Ithaca, Cornell University Press, 1976, p. 123–163.

Law

ประเสริฐ ณ นคร (เรียบเรียงเป็นภาษาปัจจุบัน) "มังรายศาสตร์" กรุงเทพฯ 2514 พิมพ์เนื่องในงาน พระราชทานเพลิงศพ หลวงโหตรกิตยานุพันธ์ (อาสา โหตรกิตย์).

A. B. Griswold / Prasert na Nagara. "The Judgments of King Maṅ Rāi." *Journal of the Siam Society*, vol. 65.1, 1977 p. 137–160.

Aroonrut Wichienkeeo / Gehan Wijeyewardene. *The Laws of King Mangrai (Mangrayat-hammasart)*. Canberra: Dept of Anthropology, Australian National University, 1986.

Pharmacology

พรรณเพ็ญ เครือไทย "มหาพนตำรา" สถาบันวิจัยสังคม มหาวิทยาลัยเชียงใหม่ 2543.

Histories

พระยาประชากิจกรจักร์ "เรื่องพงศาวดารโยนก" กรุงเทพฯ ร.ศ. 126 (พ.ศ. 2540; พิมพ์หลายครั้ง).

ฮันส์ เพนธ์ "ประวัติความเป็นมาของล้านนาไทย" สถาบันวิจัยสังคม มหาวิทยาลัยเชียงใหม่ 2526 (²2532).

สรัสวดี อ๋องสกุล "ประวัติศาสตร์ล้านนา" มหาวิทยาลัยเชียงใหม่ 2529 (22539) อมรินทร์พริ้นติ้ง แอนด์พับลิชชิ่ง จำกัด, ³2544).

Hans Penth. "Buddhist Literature of Lān Nā on the History of Lān Nā's Buddhism." *Journal of the Pali Text Society*, vol. 23, 1997, p. 43–81.

Dictionaries

อุดม รุ่งเรืองศรี "พจนานุกรมล้านนา–ไทย" กรุงเทพฯ มูลนิธิแม่ฟ้าหลวง / ธนาคารไทยพาณิชย์ จำกัด 2534, 2 เล่ม (²2547).

อรุณรัตน์ วิเชียรเขียว และคณะ "พจนานุกรมศัพท์ล้านนา เฉพาะคำที่ปรากฏในใบลาน" เชียงใหม่ สำนักพิมพ์ซิลค์เวอร์ม, 2539.

Encyclopedia

"สารานุกรมวัฒนธรรมไทย ภาคเหนือ" กรุงเทพฯ 2542 (15 เล่ม).

Website

http://www.e-lanna.com